FINDING MYSELF

How DNA and Genealogy
Changed my Life

By JenniferRose Davis

This book is dedicated to:

all the adoptees searching for their family and families searching for their loved ones.

all my generations after me, you now know.

my eighteen-month-old self, you will be okay. Live and do not regret anything about your life. You are more than just an adoptee, you are Jennifer – a daughter, mother, wife, granddaughter, sister, aunt, cousin, and friend, but most importantly, you are God's child. Your life holds value and purpose, and one day, you will know why God chose you for this journey. Follow your heart, and you will find what is missing. Mahal Kita (I love you in Tagalog).

Introduction

Life from birth to eighteen months old is a blur; it's as if it's lost in a realm of memories with someone that holds the key.

At eighteen months old, who knew that my life as a baby would change forever? My life started over at eighteen months, but I would not know my purpose in life until forty years later. *God knew* that my life was part of a bigger purpose, *a perfect plan*; God had designed specifically for me.

Baby Girl

I was born JenniferRose Davis Malaga E___, at Subic Bay Naval Hospital in the Philippines on April 10, 1976. My features were different; I had brown eyes, brown hair, and my melanin was darker than most other Filipino babies.

My birth mother, Rosalina (Rosie), was a beautiful young Filipina who lived in Olongapo City, Philippines. Like most Filipinos, Rosalina valued family, respect, and dignity.

Rosalina was born in a nearby province, San Roque, Legazpi City. At an early age, Rosalina's mother, Lourdes, left Rosalina and her two siblings, Inocentes Jr., and Rosana, to be raised by their father, Inocentes Senior.

Growing up without her mother, Rosalina eventually moved to Manila to live with her uncle. However, after discovering that her uncle was an alcoholic, she ran away and moved to Olongapo City to live other with family members.

While in Olongapo City, Rosalina had a son, Steven, in 1974. She and Steven lived with her aunt and uncle, Norma and Rolando. Her uncle worked at the local naval base.

In 1975, Rosalina met and married a young American sailor, Russell, who was in the U.S Navy. Russell left for sea duty in July 1975. He would send some financial support, but this eventually stopped around January 1977, and Rosalina never heard from Russell again. Her marriage to Russell only lasted a year.

Rosalina would later meet a Black sailor in a nearby town, Angeles City. After a brief relationship with the sailor, the two parted ways, never to see each other again. Shortly after, Rosalina would discover she was pregnant. Consequently, she gave birth to me at the local naval hospital.

Since Rosalina was still married to Russell at the time of my birth, Russell was listed as my "legal" father on my birth certificate. I would carry Russell's last name for the next eighteen months. Russell never knew this, and our lives would never cross paths, or so I thought.

After my birth, Rosalina had another baby girl in 1978 she named Maryann. With the support of her extended family, Rosalina was able to take care of her children as a single parent.

I remained with Rosalina for my first eighteen months until she realized she could no longer take care of me. She had done her best for to care for the first few months of my life. However, being single with three children was hard for Rosalina as young a Filipina.

Rosalina took me to a local orphanage in hopes of giving me a better life. She gave me up for adoption, something quite common for some single Filipinas during this period in Olongapo City, Philippines.

There were many unanswered questions about my early life. What was I like as a baby? I often wondered what the first hours of my life were like; the first words I spoke or the first step I took.

And what about Steven and Maryann, were they also given up for adoption? What happened to them. Would we ever see each other again, or would an adoptive family keep us siblings, together?

JenniferRose Davis

The Orphanage

"The greatest glory in living lies not in never falling, but in rising every time we fall." -Nelson Mandela

D uring the first eighteen months of a child's developmental stage, they may begin to discover more things beyond motor and verbal skills; they may rapidly start to increase their cognitive abilities.

We now know that children at this age may be understanding ten times more than they can put in words. A child at this age is beginning to realize they are their own person, not just an extension of their parent(s). They learn that a person can leave; however, they have not yet grasped the reality of that person not coming back.

On October 27, 1977, twenty-five-year-old Rosalina left me at a Philippines orphanage. She signed official papers that placed me in the care of King Fil-Am Home, Inc., an American owned Catholic orphanage in Olongapo City, Philippines, founded by Nun, Arlene B. Dunn, and co-founder Merle A. Andrade.

While placed in the government's guardianship, the Department of Social Welfare and Development of the Philippines, my life would change. The department would be responsible for finding a permanent placement for me through adoption. For me to thrive would be dependent on finding a good family home with lots of love and stability.

The orphanage's mission was "to organize, establish, maintain, manage, and operate for the care, support, education, and nurture of indigent deserted, or abandoned Filipino or Fil-Am children who need care and special attention.

The orphanage's vision was, "We Care – for unfortunate little ones who are deprived of parental care, provisions and the heritage of a home, therefore, We Share – not only home, love and care, but most especially the Catholic nurture and training which will develop the best in them, and We Believe – our education policies will interest you."

The ancestors watched as the connection and bond between my birth mother and child were split; our connection severed. The life I had known with my birth mother would be gone forever, and now I go on without her. Much like **two roads diverged**, our lives were going in different directions, our roads going on different paths.

My security, familiarity, and belongingness were altered, somewhat affecting my psychological development as I got older.

Choosing to give a child up for adoption may be one of the hardest things a parent ever had to do. A person may feel the thoughts and guilt for abandoning their child or constantly questioning if they made the right decision.

This process can be challenging for a parent but knowing that their child will be in a better place, hoping that their child will receive enough food, education, and better living conditions, may provide them with some comfort.

Did Rosalina say goodbye as she left me at the orphanage, or had she told me that I deserved a better life and to be with a family who could take care of me? Did she worry that I might get mistreated? Did she immediately regret her decision as she turned and walked way? Could Rosalina have stopped at any time and changed her mind, or did she want to forget about me?

That very moment in my life, at eighteen months old, would be buried deep within my thoughts and memories of Rosalina. My memory of her would eventually fade away; I would not remember anything about who she was or what she looked like. The *ties that bind* us together were now broken, and my memory of my birth mother would be lost forever.

As I was handed into a stranger's arms at the orphanage, I could not have known this would be the last time I would see my mother. I probably watched her walk away, wondering where she was going and when she was coming back. She may have looked at me for the last time, unsure if she made the right decision.

Staff at the orphanage documented in my records that I was very "sickly" when I first arrived. The doctors reported that I had terrible allergies and had broken out with a rash. I appeared malnourished; my stomach protruded. I had lice, and my hair was thin, stringy, and falling out. The doctor gave me medication to help with these issues.

It was unknown what had happened before I came to the orphanage or why my mother had brought me there; the staff assumed that my mother could no longer take care of me. They reported that my mother and I appeared to "not get along" because we were seen "fighting" when she brought me there.

The orphanage was a saving grace for me, it had become my new, temporary home until an approved adoptive family could be found. Time was of the essence. I would be cared for by nuns and staff at the orphanage, along with other children who were there waiting to be adopted.

This new place had become a **_familiar, yet unfamiliar_** place. Children in the orphanage looked like me, sounded like me, and had similar stories like mine. While some children had been there for a long time, others filtered through quickly, going to their forever home.

The longer I remained in the orphanage and the older I got, the less possibility that I would be adopted. Most families weren't looking to adopt older children. If I wasn't adopted, I would eventually be released from the orphanage to look for work or beg on the streets in a local village or nearby city.

The "age out" of the orphanages in the Philippines at that time was sixteen; human trafficking and child labor were very prevalent during that time and are still a major issue in the Philippines. "The Philippines has over 1.8 million abandoned children." The Philippines Child and Youth Code mention the child being one of the nation's most important assets, or that molding a child's character starts at home with strong family ties and their right to a wholesome family." It's obvious that children were not this country's priority.

Over the next few weeks, this place is where my potential family would first notice me. They were from the United States and was stationed at the local base, Clark Air Force Base, in the Philippines. My potential adoptive mother, Lynn, had been told about this orphanage by one of the individuals who she knew at the missionary.

The potential family was leaving the Philippines soon, and they desired to adopt another child. They had already adopted two boys, Reginald (Reggie) and Michael (Mike), from the states (North Carolina), and they were now interested in adopting a girl. However, I was not their first choice.

This family wanted to adopt a little girl they had seen at the orphanage. The girl's brother had been adopted; however, the brother's adoptive family wrote a letter to the orphanage wanting to adopt his sister, and they returned shortly after adopting the brother to adopt the sister.

The potential family came back to adopt the sister, but she was gone. They then chose to adopt me; the legalities of my adoption were sorted out so I could go home with my new family and travel to the states. My adoption would happen quickly, without much difficulty, primarily due to the orphanage's dire need for funding to remain open.

While I waited for the adoption to be finalized, the family visited me at the orphanage often. I was mostly quiet and shy. I was often in the corner playing by myself.

My brother played with me with they visited me at the orphanage. My new brother, Mike, would always try to talk to me, and he was determined to get me comfortable enough to talk to him, but I would always start screaming and crying.

At eighteen months, I had already displayed some resiliency in my life, but I was too young to understand what was happening or what "adoption" really meant. The word adoption had so much significance in my life already.

I knew my mother had left and had not come back, but where was she now that this family wanted to take me home? I was quickly learning to navigate life and that there was no way to avoid change.

Adoption

"If you don't like something, change it. If you can't change it, change your attitude." -Maya Angelou

On March 7, 1978, my life would change forever. My adoption was finalized, and the Board of Trustees of King Fil-Am Home, Inc. "agreed to release the girl child, JenniferRose Davis Malaga F., born April 10, 1976, to M/Sgt. and Mrs. E. Davis, Clark Air Force Base, R. P."

Everything about my life before this day would change forever. I was adopted into a forever home to adoptive parents who already loved and wanted me. It was like I was getting a new life, a new beginning.

Adoption can be a confusing topic for those unfamiliar with the process. Why would parents choose to adopt or place their children up for adoption? What does the process involve? How does adoption change the lives of those affected by it? And maybe the biggest question of all: What does adoption mean?

While these are essential questions, adoption has no one unique answer. Because the word adoption means different things for different people, even those who are not directly affected by it.

The definition of adoption is the action or fact of legally taking another's child and bringing it up as one's own or the fact of being adopted. To understand the meaning of adoption, talk to an adoptee, adoptive parents, or birth parents; each will have a different meaning of adoption.

For many adoptees, adoption means hope and the chance at a better life with a loving family, but unfortunately, not all children are adopted into loving families. This could also mean a place to live with no emotional connection to the adoptive family.

The meaning of adoption can also depend on one's own experience. Adoption can also mean different things at different stages of children's lives. Still, adoptees eventually respect the unselfish, difficult decision their parent(s) made to ensure they had the best chance at a better life.

Adoption for birth parents could be one of the most complex decisions they ever have to make. There are many reasons why birth parents place their children for adoption.

Maybe the parents are unable, underage, not ready or able to provide the life they know their child deserves. No matter the decision, the act of a parent(s) willingness to give their child up for adoption displays the unconditional love that a parent has for their child. It does not mean that they do not love them or want them, but that they love them so much that they are willing to do the unselfish act of allowing their child to be raised by someone else to have a chance at a better life.

Adoption for an adoptive parent(s) usually always means they want to adopt out of love. We often do not know the true reason adoptive parent(s) choose to adopt and not have biological children. Still, some adopt due to medical reasons or issues that cause them not to birth a child, while others choose to help provide a child less fortunate with a safe, secure, and loving home.

Some adopt children for other reasons. Whatever the reason, adoptive parents are a blessing and take up the slack, where parents left off and try to provide that child with some normality, unconditional love, and support throughout the rest of the child's life.

I was officially adopted and given the best gift a child could get, a loving family who wanted a daughter. God was looking out for me as He found the perfect home for me, and a baby girl for this beautiful family.

My new first name was changed to Jennifer, and Rose now became my middle name and not just a part of my first name. I would carry this name for the rest of my life, and it was special because although I did not have her (Rosalina), I had the name she had given me.

It was if my life was starting over at eighteen months old. My new adoptive family included my father, Ed, my mother Lynn, and my two older brothers, Reggie, and Mike, who were six and seven years older than me. I also had a new grandmother, Queen, and an uncle, Lee, waiting to meet me in the United States.

My father, who was born in Virginia and grew up in New York, was a Master Sergeant in the United States Air

13

Force, and my adopted mother previously served in the Air Force as well. She grew up in Arkansas, volunteered with the Chaplin's missionary on base.

We lived on the air force base in the Philippines until plans were made for us to leave for the states. The love from my new family was unconditional, and they were excited to have me as a part of their family which made their family complete.

We stayed in the Philippines for about six more months to allow the rest of the legal process to finalize, which would enable me to travel to my new home in the states. There was testing and paperwork that still had to be completed. Eventually, I was given a new Philippines birth certificate that listed my new adopted parents' names as my parents. It was as if everything about my previous identity was erased.

As I settled in with my new family, I adjusted to my surroundings. They knew that I would eventually become familiar with everyone, I wouldn't talk to them for a long time, and they weren't sure if I could speak English.

The family waited until I was ready to talk to them on my own. My mother stated that she knew I could understand Tagalog (a language spoken in the Philippines) because she saw me communicating with the house girl (maid), Emma, who spoke Tagalog to me all the time.

One day while walking on the sidewalk with Emma, I started running toward my mother yelling, "Mama, Mama, Mama!" That was the first time my mother had heard me speak to her, and she was so happy to hear me call her mama

JenniferRose Davis

Queen

"Life is about change. Sometimes it's painful.
Sometimes it's beautiful. But most of the time, it's
both." – Lana Lang

G oodbye Philippines, hello America! One thing that remained constant in my life was change, which I quickly learned that I had no control of at an early age. Change was inevitable.

Change is a movement through three phases, current, transition, and future state, and current change always seemed to be lurking around the corner. This time change would affect my everything, my surroundings, culture, religion, and home.

In 1978, I left the motherland with my new family and began my new life in the United States of America. Many Filipinos dreamed of going to the United States to start a new life, and now I was about to live this dream.

Our family flew across the waters to our new home in Florida, USA. I was leaving the PI's (Philippines Islands) behind, the only place I had ever known and whatever memory I had left of my birth mother. Did Rosalina ever imagine that I would leave the Philippines when she gave me up at the orphanage?

The Air Force transferred my father to an air force base in Florida, where my mother remembers taking me on walks on the beach. However, shortly after arriving in Florida, she and my father separated.

My father, who had previously been stationed at Castle Air Force Base, in Atwater, remarried and moved to Houston, Texas, to start a new family. He adopted his wife's daughter, Robbie.

After my parents separation, my mother, brothers, and I moved to Atwater, California, where my grandmother, Queen, lived. My grandmother was excited to have her daughter and grandchildren live close by, and she accepted me wholeheartedly as her new and only granddaughter.

Queen was born in 1923 to Harvey (Shine) and Ozie Willis (Big Mama) in Waldo, Arkansas. I had many great things about my great grandparents, but they had passed away before I could meet them. I even met Deborah, who had her ears pierced by Big Mama when she was child, and my cousin, Eugene, always talked about eating Big Mama's delicious meals.

Queen never stopped learning and pushed herself to her full potential with a limited education. She was an intelligent, hardworking, and independent who lived her life to the fullest.

My grandmother was the matriarch of our family! She was one of the oldest living relatives of the Willis family. To me, she was just my grandmother, but she was known as "Sister Babe" to the world.

Queen married, divorced, and had two children, Lynn and Lee. She relocated to Peoria, Arizona, a place she had spent many summers with her father, and she later moved to Firebaugh and Atwater, California, where she lived for many years.

My grandmother had strong southern roots and morals. When she was younger, she was sometimes referred to as "mean," which meant she didn't take "any mess" from anyone. She was fierce, a bit feisty at times, and she was not afraid to say what was on her mind. She spoke her truth, and it did not matter what anyone had to say about it.

Later in life, my grandmother dedicated her life to Christ, and from then on, she tried to live her life according to the bible. She was God-fearing and knew the bible like the back of her hand. She was always ready to argue her point when it came to the word of God, especially if it was something she believed in, and she wasn't afraid to call you out on it if she felt like you were wrong.

While in California, my grandmother helped care for my two older brothers and me while my mother worked. My earliest memories of being at her home include playing with her German Shepherd, Bobby, watching her "daytime stories" (soap operas), and picking fruit with her in the orchards.

My grandmother's undeniable love for God kept her going each day, and she enjoyed spending time with her church family teaching God's word. She served as a Sunday school and bible study teacher; she was also on the Missionary Board and sang in choir.

Queen was a devout Christian and a faithful church member, which meant that we were always at church when the doors were opened. We attended Mount Olive Baptist Church every Sunday and other church activities throughout the week; sometimes, it seemed like we were at church all day.

My mother and grandmother tried to instill Christian values in us at an early age. One Sunday, while at church, my two brothers and I marched together down the middle aisle of the church to join the church during the Invitation of Discipleship. I was about three years old, and my mother had tried to stop me from going, but I kept walking because I was going with my brothers.

The Pastor, Reverend Tyler, said since my brothers and I answered all the questions correctly, we could join the church. Not long after, we were baptized together.

I remember another time when my grandmother cooked a delicious dinner for the family, including cooking my brother's pet duck, Quincy. We all sat around the dinner table, unknowingly eating Quincy for dinner. However, there was always a lesson or meaning behind anything that she said or did, and this time, she taught us that sometimes sacrifices are made to ensure that life goes on.

My grandmother loved being outdoors and would sometimes work in her garden all day. She was strong and could do just about anything some men could do. Her hobbies included reading the bible, cooking, and fishing at her favorite fishing spots.

Often, you would find my grandmother sitting by the side of the road on a bucket fishing in a big straw hat on a pond. She would always come back and clean and fry up the fish she caught or freeze the fish to cook later.

Eventually, my grandmother decided to leave California to move back to her hometown in Arkansas to help care for elderly relatives. She sold her home, packed up her things, and rented a moving van. Once in Arkansas, she built a new home and reestablished herself in the hometown she grew up in.

My grandmother's relocation created change in all our lives. With my father and now my grandmother gone, my mother, being a single parent, tried raising us the best she could.

Family, Not by Blood

"A journey of a thousand miles begins with a single step." – Lao Tzu

L ife as I knew it was perfect in the eyes of a little girl. I had everything I needed, a family, unconditional love, and a stable home. God had placed this loving family in my life to allow me the most secure and loving upbringing.

Although my father had started a new life with a new family, he never forgot that he adopted and promised three children a chance at a better life. He was present in our lives as much he could.

My brothers and I mostly talked to our father on the phone. He and his new wife made sure to send us gifts every birthday and holiday. He visited us in California when I was six years old; I remember going to the movies to watch the new film E.T with him.

As I got a little older, I finally visited my father in Texas during the summer of my 6th-grade year. I remember being excited to see Houston for the first time and spend time with my father. The trip to Texas was the first time I flew on an airplane alone.

While visiting Texas, I got to know my stepmother, Ms. Belinda, and my stepsister, Robbie. Robbie and I were the same age; she was about six months older than me. Ms. Belinda tried her best to make me feel at home; she planned a lot of activities for us to do, including visiting Hanna–Barbera Land in Houston. She even took me to my very first hair salon appointment.

At the end of my visit to Texas, my father asked me if I would like to live with him in Texas, and I said yes. I did not know if I wanted to move to Texas, but I couldn't tell him no. He then asked my mother to allow me to stay in Houston for the school year, but she said no, and I was on the next plane back to California.

I returned to California to start my 7th grade school year at a local Catholic School, St. Anthony's School. My mother had decided to pull me out of public school to try a new school. I felt sad that I would not continue with the friends I had been with from elementary to junior high school. However, one of my best childhood friends, Andrea, attended St. Anthony's, so starting a new school alone wasn't so bad.

My mother continued working and started college, my two older brothers were left to look out for me; however, they often spent time hanging out with their friends. My mother tried hiring someone to babysit me, but I mostly spent time with a Hispanic family, Theresa (Tootsie) and Johnny, and their grandchildren, Andy and Andrea, who lived across the street from us.

Andrea became my best childhood friend; we connected instantly and spent almost every day together. Andrea's grandfather, Johnny, became somewhat of like a grandfather figure to me since I never had one before, and Tootsie stepped in my grandmother's role, whom I was missing so much.

Andrea's family treated me as if I were a part of their family, and I was always welcomed in their home. We often played together with her brother, Andy, and we had become so close that sometimes it seemed like I spent more time at their house than my own.

We enjoyed watching scary movies and Tootsie would take us to rent horror movies. At one point, we thought we had watched all the horror movies, in Big D's Video Store. Now I know where I get my love for horror flicks from

One of our favorite pastimes was "jumping the fence." Andrea's great-grandmother lived on the street behind her home, and we would often race to jump the fence in Andrea's backyard instead of walking around the corner. There was a skill to jumping the fence that we all had mastered.

Over the years, I realized that Andrea and Andy could relate to things I had gone through. Their mother, Darlene, live in another town. It wasn't until we were a little older that we learned about each other's lives.

I knew that Andrea's grandparents, Tootsie and Johnny, had adopted Darlene, and she had left Andy and Andrea in the care of their grandparents when they were younger. I also knew that Andy and Andrea had never met their father, but their grandparents knew who he was and where he was from.

Darlene had later become addicted to drugs, she would often come and go; however, she remained a constant part of their lives, especially on special occasions. We would also sometimes travel to Fresno to see Darlene., who was often homeless.

In 1985, Andrea's grandfather suddenly died of a heart attack which left their family heartbroken. Tootsie was left to raise her grandchildren on her own. This tragic event would not only alter Andy and Andrea's innocent and sheltered lives, but it would also test Tootsie's willingness to continue what she and Johnny had sought out and promised to do years before, which was to love, care and provide a safe environment for Darlene's children to grow up in.

Tootsie's love for their grandchildren was unconditional and never wavered. She did her best to continue to raise Andy and Andrea on her own. My mother made sure to be there for Tootsie whenever she needed help.

Andrea's family remained a big part of my life, we had so many great childhood memories together. However, as teenagers often do, we grew apart as we got older.

As we were both entering high school, making new friends, and trying new things, we moved on in different paths. Although we remained close friends, we stay in touch as much as we could, and I couldn't to hang out with Tootsie as often as I could.

Finding Myself

Naturalized

"Every new beginning comes from some other beginning's end." – Seneca

In 1989, this change would be one of the greatest gifts I would ever receive, in addition to being my adoption. At age thirteen, I didn't know exactly what was happening, but I knew it had to be good.

After arriving at the courthouse in Fresno, California, I rushed into a room full of people. We were called up to the front and given a certificate to sign. A judge started giving a speech at the front of the room while two men holding the American and California flag walked down the middle aisle.

The man in the front of the room instructed us to stand up, raise our right hand and recite the Oath of Allegiance. I had known the Pledge of Allegiance since we recited it daily at school, but this time was different. Why here, why now? However, I placed my hand over my heart and said the Pledge with pride along with everyone else in the room.

After everything was over, I asked my mother what this all meant. She replied, "this means you are being granted citizenship of the United States." She explained that although I was born in the Philippines, I am now a Naturalized US citizen, which would provide me many opportunities as a citizen. At the time, I did not realize what all of that meant, but I knew it was essential and something I should be proud of.

At that time, children who were adopted by U.S. citizen obtained lawful permanent resident status and automatically acquired citizenship. If the adopted child met all the conditions of INA 320 before the child's 18th birthday, the family could file Form N-600 with a fee to obtain a Certification of Citizenship, a Naturalization certificate.

As I got older, I realized that becoming a naturalized citizen was important. It was a privilege many people risked their lives and died for, and servicemembers fought to allow me and others to have this right. What was funny is that I did not even realize I was not a citizen until the Naturalization ceremony, but now, I was truly proud to be an American.

Becoming a Naturalized Citizen meant that I had the right to vote, access better education and jobs, and be eligible for money or grants. My rights would include the freedom to express myself, to worship as I wish, to a prompt, fair trial by jury, to vote in elections, to apply for federal employment, or run for elected office. It included the freedom to pursue "life, liberty, and happiness."

As stated in the Constitution: **The 14th Amendment: All persons born or naturalized in the United States, and subject to the jurisdiction thereof, are citizens of the United States and the State wherein they reside. No State shall make or enforce any law**

which shall abridge the privileges or immunities of citizens of the United States; nor shall any State deprive any person of life, liberty, or property, without due process of law; nor deny to any person within its jurisdiction the equal protection of the laws. ("Constitution of the United States," art. 1, sec.4)

Now that I had lawfully entered the USA as a Filipino citizen after my adoption, I received something many Filipinos desire, a chance for better life in the US. And as I carried my new title with pride, I became more interested in learning more about my life prior to being adopted.

I knew I was born in the Philippines and adopted. I also knew I had a mother and father somewhere, but I did not know where or why I was not with them. At that moment, I had promised myself that I would find out more about what happened and how I ended up being adopted.

JenniferRose Davis

The Box

"You will face many defeats in life, but never let yourself be defeated." - Maya Angelou

Until this point in my life; everything was seemed great. I was happy to reunite with my friends at public school my 8th-grade year at Mitchell Senior School.

My mother often talked to me about my adoption; however, she noticed I never really asked her any questions being adopted. She wasn't sure why I didn't ask questions. Although she was open with me about my adoption, I felt I didn't want to hurt her feelings by seeming curious about my birth mother.

One day, I was snooping around my mother's closet while she was at work. I notice a tin box on the shelf at the top of her closet. The box had a bunch of files and papers inside that seemed important, and my curiosity got the best of me.

As I looked through the documents, I realized that these were papers about me. I saw my name and my birth date, and I was looking at my birth certificate from the Philippines, that listed another name for my mother.

As I viewed the certificate more closely, my eyes zeroed in on the section that listed my mother's name, it read Rosalina Malaga A. I could not believe I had discovered my birth mother's name. I now had a name to go with a face I couldn't remember.

Not only did the document list Rosalina's name, but it also listed my father's name as Russell, who was listed as Caucasian. Who were these names listed as on this paper? I had suddenly become more interested about my adoption.

The paper also revealed my birth parents' birthplace, age, and address. I was shocked at all the information I had just discovered; I did not even know what to do with it. I wondered if this would be my only chance at seeing this information, so I tried to memorize as much as I could.

I dug further into the box and found more papers related to my adoption. I discovered the name of the orphanage I lived at and information about what my birth mother had reported to the agency when she had taken me there. My birth mother had reported that she was pregnant by her "Black boyfriend."

At the bottom of the file box, I found a couple of black and white photos of me as a baby. I also found passports for my brothers and me. The more information I found in the box, the more questions I had about my life in the Philippines.

I had no idea that my mother held the key to all the information about my birth mother and adoption. I was excited to find this information, but I knew I should not have gone through my mother's things without her permission. I was afraid to ask her about the information I had found, and I decided I would never tell her what I had found in the box-.

Down South

"The purpose of our lives is to be happy."
—Dalai Lama

During the summer of my 9th-grade year, I traveled with my cousins from California to Arkansas, to visit my grandmother, Queen. This was my first time traveling such long-distance road trip in a car and the first time seeing my grandmother since she had moved away.

When we first arrived in Waldo, everything seemed greener than California, the trees and grass. As we drove in, I immediately noticed a big water tower with the word "Waldo" written across it. There was a small convenience store and a gas station with a big cow on the roof called the Dairy Treat.

As drove further through town, and I noticed lots of trees, dirt or gravel roads, and old, dilapidated buildings that were probably once a vibrate downtown area. Some of the homes looked small, yet cozy. I noticed there weren't many streets with sidewalks.

The town had one grocery store, Given's, a small bank, City Hall, three gas stations, and a few other small businesses. There were no signal lights in town, only a blinking warning light. Railroad tracks ran

37

through the middle of the town, separating one side of the town from the other, and the sound of a train approaching seemed to echo in the distance.

As we approached my grandmother's home on a small street, I saw a cute little pink house surrounded by flowers and a white picket fence. There was a big porch and a concrete walkway that led to the side of her house. My grandmother met us outside and welcomed us as we parked the car.

It was awkward being in a new place without my mother, but my grandmother helped me get settled in her home. Her home was cozy, and the smell of the dinner lingered throughout the house. My new bedroom was decorated with some of her old quilts, porcelain figurines, and old pictures of her family.

I looked outside the back window of my new room and noticed a chicken coop full of chickens in the backyard. She also had a rooster that I would eventually get to know very well as he woke me up in the wee hours of the morning crowing, every day.

Over the next few days, I got to know my new home well. My grandmother was always busy working around the house, either cutting wood or messing around in her "smokehouse," looking for items. She loved to cook just about every day, and she would often share her meals with people in the neighborhood. She also enjoyed working in her garden.

She attended her family church, St. John Baptist Church in Waldo, and just as she had in California, she was a faithful member, always attending services throughout the week. She had a particular spot in the very first pew, and it was hard not to notice her head bopping from side to side when she fell asleep during church service.

My grandmother was a lady of many hats. One of her roles in the church was to collect the building fund every Sunday during the offering. After the collection plate was passed around, she would count and announce the money collected for the building fund in front of the congregation.

I will never forget one Sunday morning my grandmother stood up in front after collecting the building fund and got confused about the amount of money received. She began arguing with one of the church members about the amount, and after becoming frustrated, she yelled out, "Well, I got four monies!" At that moment, she realized she had miscounted and corrected herself, blurting out, "Shit!" and everyone in the church, including my grandmother and the Pastor, began laughing.

While visiting my grandmother over the summer, my mother decided that I would stay in Arkansas for my 9th-grade school year. I was sad that I wouldn't attend high school with friends from California. However, I was excited to be starting high school with the friends I had made in Waldo.

So far, I adapted to change well , and after my 9th-grade year, I returned to my mother in California in

JenniferRose Davis

1991. I was happy to be reunited with my peers to start the 10th grade at Atwater High School.

While my mother continued working, she transferred to Fresno State University to pursue her degree in Counseling. This left a lot of free time on my hands while she was away throughout the day. She would leave early in the morning for work and return late at night from school, leaving Tootsie and my brothers to watch over me.

I took advantage of the fact that my mother was gone all day, and I was up to no good. I hung out with my friends and my new boyfriend, Derrick, I ditched school, attended parties, snuck on to the local air force base and walked around town with my friends.

I looked forward to attending the upcoming Sadie Hawkins dance at school with Derrick. However, my friend, Lee, and I decided that we needed matching outfits for the dance, instead matching outfits with our dates. We headed to the local mall, and instead of buying our outfits, we chose to steal them off the rack. As soon as we took the items and walked out of the store, workers ran after us, detained us, and called the police.

This was the first time I had ever stolen anything, and I was embarrassed as I watched myself on video at the store. The police eventually released me to my friend's sister since my mother was not available at the time. I made sure not to mention what had

40

happened to my mother, thinking I could get away with it without her knowing.

Over the next few weeks, I continued with life as if nothing had happened and tried to keep my mother from finding out that I got caught stealing. I never mentioned it to her, but a letter came in the mail regarding juvenile hall not long after. This was the beginning of the end of my time in California.

Getting caught stealing was the last straw for my mother; she dealt with my bad behavior and was fed up. She could no longer supervise me while trying to work and finish college, and she decided that it would be best that I return to Arkansas to live with grandmother.

I tried pleading with mother to let me stay and give me another chance; I did not want to leave my boyfriend and friends, but she was not changing her mind. The decision had been made; I would finish my 10th-grade year in Waldo, Arkansas.

I waved goodbye to my mother at the Merced Greyhound bus station. I was leaving California for what I thought was for good. For a second, I thought, what if I get off the bus after she leaves and hides at my friend's house, but I was afraid of what my mother might do when she found out.

Traveling alone on a bus at sixteen years old was terrifying at first. The bus was crowded and smelled terrible. Almost every seat on the bus was taken as I walked down the narrow aisle looking for an empty seat. The bus was full, and there was only one seat left. I felt everyone staring at me as I sat down, probably wondering why I was traveling alone at such a young age.

The last empty seat was next to a Black man who was sitting in the seat near the window. I was hoping that he would give up the window seat so I could sit there, but he didn't. He didn't seem happy that I was about to take the open seat next to him.

This man was very intimidating, and he seemed cold and expressionless. He was large man, buff, and his body and arms were so big that he almost took up two seats. His demeanor said, don't mess with me. I wondered if he was a boxer or even a wrestler, but I tried not to look worried as I sat down next to him.

The man continued to listen to music on his walkman as I sat down and put my things away. I smiled at him briefly and tried not to brush up against him, but I had already bumped into him a few times while getting situated in the seat. I was waiting for him to say something to me for touching him, but he didn't.

The man must have felt my uneasiness and seen the look of worry on my face because he took off his earphones, leaned over, and whispered to me, "don't worry, you will be all right. I won't let anyone bother you." And at that moment, I felt safe, and I knew that I didn't have anything to worry about.

During the ride, we had small talk, and he eventually got off at his stop. I wish I had gotten his name to have thanked him later for making my first bus ride alone a little easier. Although he briefly crossed paths with me, I was thankful that he was there.

I was now on my own, and the bus ride was long and tiresome. I eventually made it to Magnolia, Arkansas, a town near Waldo. My grandmother was waiting to pick me up at the bus station. We drove the short distance to her home in Waldo in silence.

Over the next several months, I settled back into my grandmother's home. I was still upset with my mother about sending me to Arkansas, but I tried to make the best of it. I was back with my friends I had made in Waldo, so readjusting wasn't so bad.

One day, my grandmother tried to teach me a valuable lesson about life. We cooked one of her chickens from her chick coop for dinner, and she wanted me to do the honors.

I became terrified at the thought of killing an animal, and I began screaming and crying. She eventually killed the chicken for me and allowed me to pluck its feathers.

Although I was still traumatized by the whole event, I appreciated her willingness to teach me about life. Once again, the lesson was that sometimes sacrifices are made to ensure life goes on.

My grandmother also tried to teach me how to cook, but I refused to learn. Instead, I wanted to play outside. She told me I would one day marry a man who wanted a woman who knows how to cook. She made the best-smothered pork chops, greens, fried chicken, black eye peas, cabbage, and more. She even taught me how to make hot water cornbread.

Shortly after moving to Waldo, my brother Reggie came to live with my grandmother and me. He had been living with our father and stepmother in Houston, Texas, for a while, and I was excited to have Reggie move in with us. He was a familiar face, and I enjoyed spending time with him.

My brothers had previously visited with my grandmother for the summer for one year. They became hometown stars as they were known for their dancing skills which led to them, along with another Waldo resident, to wining 1st place in the local talent show.

In 1992, I became pregnant at age sixteen with my first child by a man I did not know much about or have a connection with. We weren't together as a couple, and his response to my pregnancy was, "It's not mine!" I was so hurt by his reaction, knowing that I would go through this pregnancy and raise my child alone.

In June 1993, at age seventeen, I gave birth to a big healthy eight-pound, five-ounce baby boy I named Carliss. I initially wanted to name him Corliss after the Arkansas Razorback basketball player, Corliss Williamson, but somehow the "a" got mixed up with the "o." And although I was young and had no idea how I was going to raise a child, I was excited about being a first-time mom.

My parents were not with me during the birth of my son, but I had plenty of support. My grandmother and our family friends, Lou Ellen and Ann, were present during the birth of my son. Ms. Lou Ellen was a nurse at the hospital; so, I was definitely in good hands.

Motherhood was such a precious thing; Carliss was the cutest baby boy with the most beautiful blue eyes that later turned hazel. He had curly brown hair and a smile that would melt anyone's heart.

As a new parent, I started thinking about my birth family more. My son was the only person biologically related to me, and I knew I would be the start of my own family tree. I wondered what it would be like to know my birth family and if they ever thought about me.

I struggled with being a single parent while still attending high school, but my family was always there for me. My grandmother helped me with my son while continuing to help raise me. I would often wonder how to teach this little guy about life when I had so much to learn about life myself.

Over the next few months, I focused on finishing high school. My grandmother, being one of my biggest supporters; helped care for Carliss while I attended school. She and my son became close and were in separatable. She tried to teach me how to be a mother, but I resisted and felt she didn't understand.

When my son was about six months old, I met Cedric, who was in the United States Army stationed at Ft. Hood, Texas. He was from Magnolia, Arkansas and would often come home on weekends on leave. Our mutual friends, Trina and Chris, introduced us while Cedric was at home one weekend.

I was always too quick to love someone without fully getting to know them, and before I knew it, I was pregnant with my second child. Although I was disappointed with myself for getting pregnant again without being married, I was excited to be having another baby.

Since Cedric was still in the military and we were not officially "together," he continued with life in Texas, and I continued with life in Arkansas. I would be graduating high school in the coming months, and I had no idea what I would do with my life or how I would support my children. I had to figure something out fast.

My high school graduation came fast, and I was excited to close this chapter in my life. I was five months pregnant at my high school graduation. My stomach was so big that I was embarrassed at the thought of walking across the stage pregnant to accept my diploma in front of an auditorium full of people.

I considered not walking at the graduation and just having my diploma mailed to me, but after talking with my friends, I decided I would walk and accept my diploma with pride. My friends encouraged me to be proud that I was able to complete high school despite being a single parent.

My parents were not able to attend my graduation ceremony, and my grandmother stayed home to care for my son, who was sick. I felt all alone knowing that my classmates were surrounded by their loved ones, and I had no one there for me. I tried to keep a smile on my face, but I was hurting deep down inside and just wanted the graduation to be over quickly.

During graduation, I remember looking out at the audience and thinking, no one will cheer for me when my name is called to receive my diploma; it will be just silence. As I heard the cheers as each of my classmates' names were called, I decided I would ask my friend if her family would cheer for me when my name was called. Her family agreed to cheer which made me feel a little better.

As I prepared to walk across the stage to accept my diploma, I focused on what I was grateful for. I was proud of myself for graduating high school as a young pregnant single parent. I had accomplished a milestone in my life, not only for me but for my son and my unborn child. I hoped my children would see that I never gave up and that you always finish, no matter what.

The Principal, Mr. Montgomery, called my name to accept my diploma, and I started what seemed like a long walk across the stage. I heard a group in the audience yell, "Jennifer!" as they clapped for me. I was

47

thankful for the support and the cheers as I accepted my diploma.

As I walked off the stage, I heard clapping and cheers from another section in the audience, and to my surprise, I saw a familiar face in the middle of the crowd. My brother, Reggie, had stood up and clapped for me as I accepted my diploma. I smiled from inside and out, knowing that someone was there for me and I wasn't alone.

After the ceremony, I looked for Reggie through the crowd and found him standing by himself, smiling at me. I ran up to him, hugged him, and thanked him for being there. My grandmother had told Reggie to "walk to the schoolhouse" for my graduation.

After graduating high school, I prepared for the birth of my second child, and in September 1994, I gave birth to my beautiful daughter, Alexis Symon'. My grandmother and our family friend, Ms. Lou Ellen, who had been at my first child's birth, were with me during the birth of Alexis.

Cedric was excited about the birth of his first daughter. Although we were not in a committed relationship, he wanted to be there for his daughter.

Cedric was not present at her birth, but he jokingly said he thinks God punished him for not being in the delivery room because the moment she entered the world, he tripped over a curb and fell flat on his face. Alexis was perfect, 6lbs and 14 oz, and now I was the mother of two beautiful children.

I did not think much about what I would do with my life. Like some people from our small town, I applied for a job and was hired at one of the local chicken plants, Hudson Foods in Hope, Arkansas, to work the night shift. I was excited about my first job but had no clue what I was getting myself into.

Working at the chicken plant for the next ten months was hard; I started as a box maker, which required little to no skills, and quickly moved on to other roles in the plant, sometimes working in the freezer with cold temperatures. I hated this job and couldn't imagine doing this job forever. I knew I wanted more in life.

Over the next few months, life continued as usual. I hadn't thought much about my birth parents; I had become so numb to my feelings of being adopted. There was always a void in my heart, as if something were missing, but I never knew what to do with my feelings, so I kept my feelings to myself.

Certain things reminded me of that void, and sometimes I wondered what it would have been like if I had been with my birth parents. I wondered who they were and if they cared about knowing what happened to me. I assumed that whoever my birth parents were, they had forgotten about me by now. I felt sad knowing that my children may never know anything about them and about our roots.

I started having questions, like how a mother could give up her child for adoption. It was hard to imagine ever giving up my children, leaving them alone, and never seeing him again. I wondered what Rosalina felt when she gave me up or what led to her decision to place me up for adoption.

Finding my birth parents seemed so farfetched to me, and I wondered how I would go about it. And if I found them, would they be happy to see me? I had accepted that I might never know anything more about that part of my life. I knew it was time to forget about them and focus on who I did have in my life, my children.

Angel on Earth

"Always remember that you are unique. Just like everyone else." -Margaret Mead

One cold winter night, I attended a party in one of the neighboring towns. The person I had come to the party with left early, and I had such a good time that I had not even considered how I was going to get home. I knew my grandmother would never agree to get up in the middle of the night with my children to pick me up, so I had to find my way home.

I left the party walking towards the highway, thinking I would hitchhike home. I knew I would not be able to walk to Waldo, and there were not many cars out that late at night. I stopped at the local gas station and sat on the curb outside the store, hoping someone would drive by. It was the first time I had ever hitchhiked!

I started to get discouraged after not seeing a single car in sight for a while. Finally, after about forty-five minutes, a grey car pulled up to the gas station. An elderly Caucasian man, who was in his late seventies or eighties, got out of the vehicle. He walked over to me and asked me if I needed help. I told him I was trying to get home to Waldo, and I needed a ride.

The man offered to take me home, but I told him that I did not have any money to give him for gas. He said, "That is okay; you do not have to pay me any money." I thanked the old man for going out of his way to take me home. He explained that he was not from this town, and he was passing through.

I was a little reluctant about getting into a stranger's car; I had seen enough scary movies about hitchhikers getting into the wrong vehicle and being murdered. However, I was carefree and fearless during that age, and I only worried that this might be my only chance at getting a ride home. I decided to take a chance.

After getting into the old man's car, I sat as far over to the door as possible, thinking I may have to jump out quickly. I held on to the door latch as tight as I could and skipped putting on my seat belt just in case I needed to react fast. I felt a little uneasy, but it was too late, and the old man had started to drive off. I sat quietly and said a quick prayer that I would make safely.

We were mostly quiet during the short ride; we had small talk. I wanted to stay alert just in case something happened. At one point, I dozed off for what seemed like a few seconds, only to jerk awake quickly to remember that I was in a strange man's car.

Before I knew it, we had pulled onto my grandmother's street, and he stopped in front of her house to let me out of the car.

I couldn't remember giving him the directions to my home, but I must have. As I got out of the car and walked away, the old man rolled his window down and told me it was dangerous to hitchhike and to be more careful next time. I agreed and continued walking.

As I made it to my grandmother's gate, I turned around to thank the old man, but he was gone. There was no sign of him or his car anywhere. I stood there bewildered, confused about how he could have left so fast. It all started to feel like a dream.

I ran the short distance to the corner of the street to see if I could see the car lights, but there weren't any lights in sight. I had stopped trying to find an explanation and accepted it for what it was, a nice old man giving me a ride home. I was happy to be home.

I never really thought about this experience again until I brought it up to a friend, Torsha, years later. I told her this was something in my life that I never could explain because I did not remember much about the ride home that night and didn't even get a chance to say thank you.

After I finished telling my story, Torsha responded, "This was your guardian angel!" I thought for a second, could this be true? My friend said, "How else do you explain that you do not remember the ride home, you made it home safely, and then you turned around, and the car was gone. God was watching over you that night." I smiled at the thought of knowing that I had seen my guardian angel, and I had not even realized it. I never questioned it again.

Over the next few months, Cedric eventually processed out of the active-duty military and moved home to Magnolia. He lived with his parents and joined the Arkansas National Guard.

Cedric was present in his daughter's life , and we talked about being a family. We decided to move in together and try to build a life together. He also stepped up as a positive influence in my son's life.

I eventually applied for jobs and got hired at Taco Bell. It was my second "real job," and I enjoyed being a working mom. Cedric's parents helped with Alexis and often took me to and from work. My grandmother continued to help me with my Carliss. I was happy to be able to contribute to the household bills.

In January of 1998, we welcomed our second daughter, I'Layia Malise, and for a while, she was the baby of our family. She was perfect with her big brown eyes and long beautiful black hair. She was a "mama's baby" and always wanted to be with me. I was in love all over again, and she made our little family complete.

On May 4, 1999, Cedric and I were married in our family friend's, Rev. Charles, home. Ms. Lou Ellen, Rev. Charles's mother, pulled strings to marry us on such short notice due Cedric was deploying the next day to Saudi Arabia. There was no engagement, honeymoon, or wedding ceremony; there was barely even a ring. We were just two young adults trying to do the right thing for our family.

During the storm, the sky was dark and gloomy, and the wind had begun to pick up. We wondered if the tornado would stop us from getting married.

54

We rushed into Rev. Charles's home, trying to avoid the storm. Sister Ann held one of my daughters in her arms and my other daughter's hand; my son was with my grandmother. Cedric and I repeated the wedding vows to each other quickly, and we were married.

I didn't know much about married life. I had nothing to compare marriage to, only Cedric's parents, and his aunts and uncles, who I had only known for a short time.

My mother and grandmother were both divorced, but I knew that marriage came with ups and downs. Cedric and I did our best as newlyweds with three children. We tried to remain committed to our marriage and work through our problems together.

In August of 1999, I decided to enroll in the local university at Southern Arkansas University. I continued to work part-time while attending college. I knew that getting my degree would open new doors for our family and provide unlimited opportunities. I was excited to be taking steps to give our family a chance at a better life.

I always wanted to pursue a career in social work because I wanted to give back what was given to me. I knew that a social worker assisted with my adoption in the Philippines, and I had hoped to be able to give back in that way.

Cedric was activated and deployed overseas three times during our marriage. I was reminded of the sacrifices he and his fellow soldiers made to our community and to our nation. I had support from family and friends, who helped our family during his deployments.

JenniferRose Davis

Searching for Rosalina

"To adoptees. Never be afraid of searching for the truth. The joy that may await you will far outweigh the burden of your long journey." — *Diamond Mike Watson*

I officially started searching for my birth mother around the summer of 2000. I wondered how I would find someone who was living in another country. I began telling my story about being adopted to anyone that listened.

The pain of realizing that I didn't know much of about my birth mother hurt. I only had the information I had seen years ago. Any memory of her I had was buried deep and I couldn't' remember her.

As I adapted to college life at Southern Arkansas University, I began spending time in the computer lab for my studies, which gave me unlimited access to the worldwide web.

I spent hours in the lab researching information about adoptions and how to find birth parents. I even signed up with different websites and read stories of successful adoption reunions. I knew having access to the internet would be essential to my search.

I woke up and went to bed thinking about how I could search and find her. There was not a day that went by that I did not somehow search for my birth mother. After going to college, working, and raising my children, any spare time I had was dedicated to searching for Rosalina. This search had started to take priority in my life.

First, I tried to remember the information listed from my adoption records and original birth certificate that I had seen years ago as a child. It had been so long ago, and I was unsure if I had the correct information. I knew Rosalina's maiden name, but I was uncertain if I had the correct spelling or if she was still married.

I read Philippines online message boards and searched for people with similar surnames from Olongapo City, Philippines. I ran across stories of people looking for loved ones and with similar last names, but after messaging them, they were not able to confirm that they knew Rosalina.

I decided to post online messages explaining that I was born and adopted in the Philippines and looking for my birth mother. I had hoped that someone would recognize my birth mother's name or my story. One lady, Ms. Cynthia, a Filipina responded, "If you never find your mother, I will be your mother."

Little did I know that I was one of the thousands of children born in the Philippines with similar circumstances; children from the Amerasian Community, also known as the "Forgotten Community."

An Amerasian included any person who was fathered by a citizen of the United States (servicemembers) and whose mother is or was an Asian National. Some Amerasians preferred the term, Fil-Am, Filipino and American.

Many of servicemembers stationed at either Clark Air Base or Subic Naval Base in the Philippines had fathered children during their time in the Philippines. Some married their children's mother and accepted their children. Some servicemembers unknowingly father children, while other knew and left the Philippines, choosing not to be involved in the child's life.

Although the United States Congress passed the Amerasian Immigration Act of 1982, which gave preferential immigration status to Amerasians children born in Korea, Thailand, Vietnam, Cambodia, and Laos during the Vietnam War, it did not include those children born in the Philippines. Former American G.I. fathers had to claim children from the Philippines for them to claim U.S Citizenship.

Amerasians in the Philippines consisted of a quarter of a million people, subjected to poverty, or had a stigma of being illegitimate children and endured prejudice due to their physical features.

I became intrigued with the Amerasian Community and started reading about life in the Philippines for Amerasians. Amerasians were often left with a negative stigma and assumed to be children of prostitutes whose father abandoned them. Some children of African

American fathers often suffered the most prejudice and were left as "street kids."

Many children were left to live in abject poverty and marginalization. These children were out of work, homeless, suffered from alcohol and drug abuse, or had familial abuse problems, as well as identity confusion and unresolved grief issues over the loss of their mothers and fathers. They may have also suffered from social isolation and low self-esteem

I was blessed to have been adopted quickly by a loving family and brought to the states. I didn't endure the disparities that other Amerasians had experienced in the Philippines. Today nearly 50,000 Amerasian remain in the Philippines.

Not long after I posted a message on a Philippines message board, I received a reply from a Filipino nurse who suggested that I contact the Philippines Vital & Statistics agency to get a copy of my birth mother's birth certificate or marriage license. She felt this information could lead me my birth mother's whereabouts.

I located the Philippines Civil Registration and Vital Statistic's website and started to complete the online application to request a birth certificate. The cost for a record was $20, such a small fee to pay that would allow me access to everything I needed to find my birth mother.

As I tried to answer the questions about my birth mother on the application, I realized I did not know the answers. I couldn't' remember what I had seen as a child on the documents in my mother's closet. I had always known that I would one day need this information, and now I had forgotten most of what I had seen.

I decided to email one of the Vital Statistics employees from their website directory about getting this information. I found a list of employees, picked one name, and emailed him asking how I would go about getting a copy of my birth mother's birth or marriage certificate with little to no information.

I received a quick response from Raul in the Philippines, who informed me that I could not request that information. He then asked why I needed this information, and I explained that I was adopted, searching for my birth mother and that I needed the information to help locate her.

Raul responded and asked me what I knew about my birth mother. I explained that I knew her name and her husband's name (the man listed on my birth certificate). I provided him with the little information I had but was unsure if I had the correct spelling. I tried to include everything I could remember from what I had seen years ago, which was not a lot. I wondered why Raul asked for this information if he could not grant my request for the records?

Raul explained in the email that he could not give me a copy of my mother's birth certificate or marriage license, but instead he included in the email her complete name (correct spelling), new married last name, birth date, her mother's name (Lourdes), and a previous address in Olongapo City. He also suggested that I search for Rosalina in the states because she had married an American named Samuel T. and had possibly moved to the U.S.

I was overwhelmed with all the information Raul provided; I knew this would be vital to my search. To finally have correct information to help me find Rosalina was like a dream come true. It took a few minutes to process the blessing I had just received. I felt like crying, but held it in.

I immediately took this information and searched online for Rosalina and her husband in the United States. I posted several messages on U.S. online message boards asking if anyone knew Rosalina or Samuel T. I also searched their names and located potential matches in a couple of states in the U.S.

A few days later, I received a reply from one of the Ancestry.com messages boards, a lady in California named Debbie B. She stated that she found information regarding Rosalina M., who divorced Russell F. in San Diego, CA. She forwarded me the information, and to my amazement, I was looking at my birth mother's information about her divorce from the man whose name was listed as my father on my on original birth certificate.

This information confirmed that I was on the right track and that Rosalina had made it to the states. Finding the divorce information was a great lead, and I felt confident that I would eventually find Rosalina.

Next, I decided I would also search for Rosalina's ex-husband, Russell, and reach out to him to see if he had any information about her whereabouts. Finding Russell's information on the internet turned out to be one of the easiest finds yet.

I knew that Russell was not my father. My birth mother mentioned she was pregnant by her "Black boyfriend" in my adoption records and Russell was listed as "White." However, finding my birth father without a name or location would be like finding a needle in a haystack.

I googled Russell's name, and there he was, his name, address, and phone number. I could not believe how easy it was to find someone in the U.S.

I decided I would call Russell, but I wondered if he would be willing to talk to me or become upset that I was asking questions about his ex-wife. Despite feeling nervous, I picked up the phone and dialed his number.

Everything was happening so fast that I had not even prepared myself about what to say if Russell answered the phone. Before I knew it, a man answered the phone. I said, "Hello, Mr. F., you don't know me, but you may remember my mother, Rosalina." There was a short pause on the other end of the line; but he finally responded by saying yes, that is my ex-wife; we're divorced. I introduced myself, and to my surprise, Mr. F. was willing to talk to me.

Mr. F told me that he did not have any information about my mother. He said that he divorced Rosalina and has not had any contact with her since he left the Philippines.

Reluctantly, I asked him if he knew anything about my birth father, and he said no. He said, "any information I did have about your mother is gone; my second wife burnt it up in a fire. His exact words regarding his second wife were, "She was a Bitch!"

I thanked Mr. F for his time and information. He said, "I'm sorry you were put up for adoption," and I appreciated him for saying that. Before we ended our conversation, Mr. F told me that he remembers Rosalina had a little boy named "Stevie or something like that" and that Stevie was always with an aunt.

I was grateful for the little information I had gotten from Mr. F, especially about Stevie. I realized I might have a brother out there. I was excited but immediately felt sadness, wondering if Stevie was adopted too. I now realized not only was I looking for Rosalina, but I was also looking for a brother, Stevie.

I continued to tell my story of being adopted to all that would listen, and people suggested that I reach out to the Jenny Jones show, a popular talk show on television during that time, to see if she could help me find my birth mother. I thought about the reunion shows I had seen on the show, and some weren't happy endings. I decided not to reach out to the talk show.

On February 1, 2000, I posted a message on a message board in the United States that said, **"I am looking for Samuel T. who married a Filipina woman in 1979 named Rosalina. Rosalina is my mother who put me up for adoption. Please respond so I can find my mother. Jennifer."**

Five days later, on February 6th, I got a response from a lady named Candy T. M. My heart skipped a beat when I saw that Candy's last name, T, was the same as Rosalina and Samuel's last name.

JenniferRose Davis

Candy

"You will face many defeats in life, but never let yourself be defeated." -Maya Angelou

Candy responded to my message, stating you have found your mother. She said Rosalina was her sister-in-law and that I could stop searching. She explained that she told Rosalina about me, and Candy asked that I give her time to process everything. I could not believe what I was reading. Could this be true, did Candy really know my birth mother?

I discovered that Candy did indeed know Rosalina. Rosalina was married to Candy's brother, Samuel. Candy insisted that I call her Aunt Candy, and our friendship began. Candy had become a true angel that connected me to my birth mother.

In September 2000, Aunt Candy wrote me twice in one day. **"Hi Jennifer, I'm so happy they finally contacted you. I talked to my brother (Mr. T) the other day, and he said they contacted you. I'm glad and hope you can see them soon. Always remember I am here for moral support and if I can help, I will. Welcome to the family. It's a bit a screw but Who's isn't. All we have is each other. Gotta go never have enough time to do anything snow on the ground today about 4in so far.**

And more on The way. Work work!!!!!! Write to me and maybe you'll be able to See them soon. Give your mom some time; she has carried a heavy burden for a long time, and giving up the reality of what she did is hard for her to accept. She'll come around a lot of it is she is ashamed and embarrassed at what she had to do. Accepting that is something I understand I still worry what will happen and how I'm going to explain to my boys why I did what I did. But some people take longer to figure it out than others. Just don't judge her right now. She's punished herself enough through the years. If you got questions about that, ask me; maybe I Can help through my own experiences. She doesn't want to talk to me about it yet either. Gotta go for sure now. Love you aunt candy. (that's what your brothers and sisters call me) hey if you don't mind Please forward my brother email to me so I can see what he said to you. just me aunt Candy Miller farms"

She also wrote, "hi again, feel ranked today I emailed you twice in one day everyone else is hollering at me to write. But you are the priority right now. The letters sound encouraging. My poor brother. he really is cool. You will like him. He's pretty down to earth. Hang in there. We'll bring your mom around. Once she sees how the rest of the family reacts, she'll warm up. I talked to her the other day and she wants me to come up there bad. I know she wants to talk. She isn't much on writing anymore, she used to be real good. That's how we met at first cause they were stationed in long beach for a year before I met her. she is sweet and kind. I'll try and call her this weekend. Don't give up on the rest of the bunch, they all have pretty busy lives too, and aren't real good at keeping in contact. Jo is my informant most of the time, she does stay in touch with me. she is a sweetheart. A lot of fun but pretty hard headed like her dad. But I get along with her well. I don't know Mimi yet, I have talked to her on the phone and they have a sweet little baby boy. But they weren't together when I was down there last. Gotta go write soon love aunt Candy

MILLER FARMS"

God had placed Aunt Candy in my life at just the right time. She had accepted me wholeheartedly, even before I had met my birth mother. Aunt Candy was so sweet and open with me about her life and family. She eventually told me she knew exactly what I was going through.

Aunt Candy stayed in contact with me, and I enjoyed reading her email updates about life on her farm in Texas or what she and her husband, Uncle Shane, had done throughout the day. We continued to email each other, and I promised her that I would visit her soon. I didn't know I would only have a short time left with Aunt Candy.

One day, the emails stopped coming; Aunt Candy had been battling cancer for the past few years and passed away on November 11, 2003. I regretted never meeting her- to thank her in person for connecting me with Rosalina.

Over the next few weeks, I patiently waited for Rosalina to reach out to me. After a few weeks went by without hearing from her, I wondered why she had not picked up the phone to call me. I thought she would be excited that I found her and would immediately call me, but she didn't. I waited and waited for her call.

I decided I would write Rosalina a letter to the address I found online while I waited for her to contact me. I wrote a heartfelt letter, with the help of my sister-in-law. I assumed Rosalina would sign for it and confirm she lived there. However, when I received the receipt, I was unable to read the signature, which left me no closer to knowing if Rosalina lived there.

While waiting for Rosalina to contact me, I received a call from a man who introduced himself as Samuel T, Rosalina's husband. I was excited to hear from him yet nervous because it was not Rosalina calling me herself. I started thinking, what if he called me to tell me that Rosalina did not want to talk to me. My heart sank, but I listened anxiously while he spoke.

Samuel explained that Rosalina knew about me but was taking a while to process everything. He told me that I had been a secret, and no one knew about me. I felt a lump in my throat, and tears began to swell up in my eyes just thinking all this time I was a secret and she had never told anyone about me.

At first, I did not know how to receive this information and my feelings were beyond hurt. I listened as he went on. He stated that Rosalina will call me but to give her time. He explained that if Rosalina did not reach out to me before the holidays (Thanksgiving), he would tell his children about me, my four half-siblings, Steven (Steve), Maryann, Samantha Jo (Jo Jo), and Samuel III (Sammy).

I was happy to recognize Steve's name from what Mr. F had told me about Stevie and to know that he wasn't given up for adoption made me happy. I was thankful that Samuel called me, and I accepted that this would not be an easy process for Rosalina and now I worried if she would accept me.

Not long after speaking to Samuel, Rosalina attempted to call me. I was so upset when I learned that I had missed her call. I did not hear my phone ring, but she left a voicemail. It was the first time I heard my mother's voice since I was a baby. I repeatedly replayed her message several times just to listen to her. It took a few days to gather the courage to call her back; I had no idea what I would say. I eventually tried calling her back, but her phone went to her voicemail.

A few days later, I received a call from Remirose (Mimi), my brother Steve's wife. I was so excited that she and Steve called me. Both Steve and Mimi seemed excited to get to know me, and they welcomed me into the family with open arms. They also invited me to come to Virginia Beach, Virginia, to meet everyone in person for Thanksgiving. I was ecstatic!

Over the next few weeks, my siblings and I got to know each. During one of our phone calls, Mimi asked me to describe myself. At first, I didn't know what to say, but

71

then I explained that I was half Black and Filipino, with brown eyes and long brown hair. As Mimi repeated this aloud, I overheard Rosalina say in the background, tell her she is not half-Black; her father is Puerto Rican.

This took me by surprise, Puerto Rican? No one ever told this before, and growing up, I had always identified with being half African American. It was never mentioned in my adoption or birth records that I was Puerto Rican. I decided to keep this knowledge until further information about my ethnicity could be confirmed or until I found my birth father.

The Clothes Hanger

"The greatest glory in living lies not in never falling, but in rising every time we fall." -Nelson Mandela

Finding and one day meeting my birth mother was something I never imagined could happen. I always knew I would search, but I never thought I would find her. It all felt surreal.

Now everything was happening so fast. I wondered what meeting my birth mother for the first time would be like and our relationship afterwards. I worried that she would not accept me as part of her family, since I had outed her secret. I had to remember that she did give me up for adoption for a reason.

I immediately started planning my trip to Virginia, and I decided I would drive there. It would be my first Thanksgiving I would spend away from my children; however, my family supported me in my decision. My husband and I decided it was best to meet everyone first on my own and take my family to meet them later.

This would also be the first time driving such a long distance by myself. However, the seventeen-and-a-half-hour trip to Virginia would allow me time to reflect on everything and prepare myself for this new chapter in my life.

The drive to Virginia started out great. I stopped at a few different places to rest and explored this side of the country I had never seen before. I was making good driving time, and I was excited my life would change forever in just a few short hours.

The drive allowed me to reflect and talk with God. I asked Him if I had made the right decisions or am I hurting my adoptive family by pursuing this relationship with my birth mother, and eventually my birth father. I asked God to give me the strength to get through this first meeting with my birth family.

I played out different scenarios in my head about what it would be like seeing Rosalina for the first time after many years. I wondered if we would both cry and hug as I had imagined so many times. I honestly did not know what to expect, but I had already started building a bond with my siblings through phone calls and emails, and I knew they would be there to support both of us.

I was on schedule with my route to Virginia, and the drive was not that bad. Time was on my side, and my sister Jo Jo stayed on the phone with me throughout my trip. As it started getting late, I decided to stop off at the next exit with a gas station.

At first, I was a little leery about stopping for gas late at night, but I knew it would be a quick stop, and I would be on my way. Besides, my gas had gone below half a tank, and I wanted to keep it above to ensure I did not run out of gas.

As I pulled up to the gas station, I noticed that it was also a truck stop with a restaurant. However, it was old, rundown, and isolated, with what looked like a sleazy motel across the street. It reminded me of the gas stations in the scary movies I watched when I was younger.

I quickly filled up my gas tank and got back in the car with no problems. I started to pull off when I realized that I should go to the restroom so I would not have to stop again. I pulled up close to the store, and as I got out of my car and locked the door, I realized my keys were still in the ignition.

I was so upset that I had just locked my keys in the car. I was in the middle of nowhere locked out of my car in the middle of the night. There was a small gap in my car door, but after I tried a few times, but the door would not open enough to unlock the door. I leaned against my car for what seemed like hours, trying to figure out what to do next.

I attempted to ask for help from a few customers going into the store, but no one could help me. As I stood around thinking about what to do, I thought someone in the store could help. I approached the cashier in the store, and he immediately pointed towards the back and told me to ask the lady in the restaurant. Apparently, he had been watching me through the window and knew I had locked my keys in the car.

I walked towards the back of the store towards the kitchen, which was covered in a smoky haze and smelled like old burnt grease. I saw a large woman through a serving window, and I asked her if she could help me unlock my car door. The woman continued what she was doing and never looked up. I said excuse me, this time asking for a clothes hanger, but she ignored me, never acknowledging that I was even there.

I was so frustrated and headed back out to my car. A man who had been getting gas walked up and asked what was wrong. The man suggested that I walk across the street to the motel and ask if I could use a clothes hanger; surely the motel would have a clothes hanger they could spare. I thanked him for his help and felt that it was worth trying.

The walk to the motel was short, but it was cold and windy. The last thing on my mind was that I was walking by myself, late at night in a strange town. My focus was on getting my car doors unlocked and getting back on the road. I had already lost three hours dealing with this ordeal, and I was upset and tired.

I walked up to the motel lobby door. The sign on the door showed "No Vacancy," although the parking lot was empty. The lobby was dark, but there was a small light on from a lamp on the front desk.

The motel seemed eerily quiet and unoccupied, but I was hopeful as I noticed an old lady sitting in a chair directly in front of the lobby door. It was as if she placed her chair there and waited for me to walk up to the door to come in.

An uneasiness came over me as I got closer to the lobby door. As I reached the door, I noticed that the lady was glaring at me. She looked almost ghostly, her face expressionless and she sat very still staring at my next move. She didn't acknowledge I was there.

I pulled on the door latch, but it didn't move. The door was locked. I waved at the lady on the other side of the door, but she did not respond. She continued to stare at me. I looked closer through the glass and asked her if the motel were open and if she had a clothes hanger I could use, but the lady never said anything. I motioned towards the lady again, but there was no response.

At this point, I felt uncomfortable and was afraid. I knew she was purposely ignoring me. I knew she was not willing to help me, I decided to go back to my car. I walked quickly, afraid to look back at the motel.

Once I made it back to my car, I wondered what I had just experienced. I tried to make sense of why the lady was at the door but would not acknowledge my presence; something was not right.

I had run out of ideas for getting my car door opened. After talking on the phone with my family, I realized I would have to wait until the morning to try and get help. It was dark and cold, but I stayed near my car, which seemed the safest place at the time.

I leaned on my car and dozed off a few times, and when I woke, a man walked up to me and asked if I needed help. I told him I had locked my keys in the car, and I was not able to get any help from anyone. I told him about my experience in the store and with the lady at the motel. He told me that I shouldn't be out here by myself and that he would help me get my car door opened so I could be on my way.

The man suggested that I ask one of the truck drivers parked at the truck stop since most were on the road; someone had to have clothes hangers. He said, "If you go up to the trucks and ask someone for a hanger, I will watch out for you and make sure nothing happens." At this point, I did not even care and I was so ready to try anything. I was willing to do whatever he asked.

Luckily, the first truck I knocked on, someone answered and handed me a clothes hanger. I felt stupid for not thinking about doing this first, it would have saved a lot of time.

I returned with the clothes hanger, and the man helped me stick the hanger through the gap in my door to unlock my car. I was so grateful that he stopped to help and thanked him several times. I almost hugged him, but I shook his hand instead.

The man told me to make sure that I never stop in this town again. He said, "You stopped in one of the most racist towns in Tennessee, and they don't like our kind here." At this point, I became afraid and vowed to never stop in Jackson, Tennessee again.

My 17-hour drive now turned into a 23-hour trip due to locking my keys in the car. The last few hours of my drive into Virginia, I stayed on the phone with my sister, JoJo. Having someone to talk to while driving helped ease my nerves about what had just happened and with meeting my family for the first time.

JenniferRose Davis

Welcome to Virginia

"Love the life you live. Live the life you love."
-Bob Marley

As I pulled up to my brother's apartment in Virginia Beach, I was excited and nervous at the same time. I had found my family, but I had also revealed Rosalina's secret, and I didn't know how she truly felt about me.

Everyone greeted me with a warm welcome, which took the edge off a little. I remember looking at everyone, wondering how I fit in; I was the only one half African American. However, I was finally with people who and shared the same blood as me, something I had only experienced with my children.

The first time I saw Rosalina, I felt like an emotional roller coaster. It was like *having unfamiliar blood* in my veins and, at the same time, still not feeling like I truly belonged there. I went from happy to see her to, sad that I had missed out on so many years and hurt that she had only given me up for adoption.

Rosalina was beautiful, like *a beautiful butterfly*. She was Filipina with long black hair and the sweetest smile I had ever seen. Her reaction to seeing me for the first time since she had left me at the orphanage was hard to read. She kept her emotions well-hidden, and there was no crying like I imagined. We hugged, and I thought I saw the pain in her eyes, but I wasn't' sure. I wondered if seeing me took her back to a place in her life that she wanted to forget.

That very moment was probably bittersweet for her. I am sure she never imagined that she would see me again when she left me at the orphanage in the Philippines. Despite all that happened, I wanted to start from now, and she seemed to want that too.

Rosalina spent Thanksgiving with us at my brother's apartment, and the rest of the family came over as well. Rosalina was mostly standoffish, at times.

I felt awkward sitting next to Rosalina on the couch because I did not know what to say. There was so much that I wanted to say and things I wanted to ask, but I knew it was not the right time.

My brother, Steve, must have sensed what I was feeling because he pulled me aside and told me to not "expect too much from mom" because she was always this way growing up. He said she never shared much with them about her life in the Philippines, and they did not know anyone from the side of the family in the Philippines.

JoJo told me the same thing; she said she thought she had seen one letter from a family member in the Philippines when she was younger, but she wasn't sure. She said mom is not the type to show her emotions.

Hearing both of my siblings say this gave me somewhat of an understanding. I didn't know what

Rosalina had gone through while in the Philippines or what had led up to her taking me to the orphanage, I accepted that this was hard for her and she may not be ready.

Although Rosalina's reaction to seeing me again was not what I expected, I tried to understand. My idea of how a mother would feel after seeing her child she had given up so many years ago seemed to be so much more than what she had shown. I know that people handled things differently, but I just hoped she was happy that I had found her.

Over the next few days, Rosalina stopped by to see me every day. The visits were short, but I was happy for our time together. My new family had shown me such great hospitality while I was there. The visit had gone well. Before I knew it, it was time to leave and return to Arkansas.

The drive home to Arkansas was very different from the drive coming. I went back home, knowing a part of my past that I thought was forever lost. I was excited about this new chapter with my birth family and what this meant for my children and their children. The drive home went well; I hadn't even noticed as I drove through Jackson, Tennessee, without stopping.

Over the next couple of years, I stayed in touch with my new family. I was content with the relationship Rosalina and I had. I talked to her on the phone a few times, and she always asked about my children, but I felt sad she has never met them. I assumed she wasn't interested in meeting my children.

I was happy to build a great relationship with my new siblings over the years. They included me and treated me as a part of the family. I was now a big sister, something I had never been before.

One day while talking on the phone Jo Jo, she attempted to try and help me find out who my father was by asking Rosalina. I heard Rosalina say, "I don't want to get him involved." I was so hurt by what I had just heard. I could not believe she knew who my father was but was not willing to tell me. Jo Jo encouraged me to continue to ask Rosalina about my father; she thought she would eventually come around and give me the information I needed to find him.

In 2003, I returned to Virginia Beach for my sister's wedding. I was excited to see everyone again; it had been a few years since first meeting them, but I truly felt like part of the family. This time, I decided to fly to Virginia instead of driving, and Steve picked me up from the airport.

I stayed with my brother, his wife, and their daughter again, but this time at the family home. Rosalina's husband, Samuel, and my younger brother Sammy also lived there, and it was nice spending time with everyone. Rosalina made sure to stop by as often as she could.

Jo Jo's wedding was beautiful. I was excited to be celebrating this special time in her life. We spent time together getting our nails, hair, and facials done before the wedding. We also had a lovely rehearsal dinner at a Japanese restaurant hosted by my brother Steve. I was excited to be making memories with my family.

My conversations with Rosalina weren't any different from the first visit. I was afraid to ask questions about my adoption. Besides, I realized Rosalina was not fully acknowledging me as her daughter, which was evident during one of our outings.

We all went to a local bar, and Rosalina said to the man at the door, remember my children I introduced to you before, and she didn't include or introduce me as daughter as well. I realized we were not in a place in our relationship to confront her with my questions, so I held back from asking once again.

I realized Rosalina, and I may never have that bond that I had longed for, and I would never have answers to the questions I had. I accepted that things were the way they were, and I decided to move on and focus all my energy on finding my father on my own.

Life Happens

"What we think, we become." - Buddha

On May 14, 2004, I graduated from Southern Arkansas University with my Bachelor of Science in Criminal Justice, a Minor in Computer Information Systems, and an Associate of Science in Business Administration. I was proud of my accomplishments; I had never imagined getting not one but two degrees.

Unlike my high school graduation, many people came out to support me. Although my husband was deployed to Iraq, my best friend, Yoshalan, my brother Reggie, my father, and stepmother, and my mother and father-in-law, were all present during my graduation ceremony. I was grateful for everyone that attended this special occasion.

After graduating college, I was promoted to Case Manager at South Arkansas Youth Services. I loved my job and enjoyed working with youth.

Cedric and I knew we wanted more for our family, which did not include staying in Arkansas. As he out-processed from the active-duty military after being deployed to Iraq, we decided to move to Texas for a fresh

87

JenniferRose Davis

start. We both loved Texas, and on July 30, 2005, we moved to Killeen, Texas, to start a new life.

Moving to Texas was one of the best decisions we had made. My husband took a military contracting position and I applied for a job with the State of Texas. I became employed as an Intake Specialist for the Department of Family and Protective Services (DFPS) abuse hotline, and after six months was promoted to CPS Investigator in Austin, TX. I eventually transferred to Killeen and took a position with the Texas Health & Human Services Commission as a Texas Works Advisor II and III.

Our family grew, and I had two more children, Jaden Kimani in 2008 and Kailani Rose in 2009. I never imagined having five children, but I loved our large family. I remember one of Cedric's older cousins whispered to my mother-in-law, "How many more children is she going to have?" My family's response was just as many as you (she had about seven or eight children).

Everything was falling into place for our family, and I felt good about moving to Texas. My husband and I had good jobs, and my children were healthy and happy. I had a great relationship with my new family, but the void was still there, the void of not knowing my birth father.

I had become consumed with my family and work, but I still had the desire to know my birth father and learn more about his side of my family. A part of me was still missing.

However, in 2009, God blessed me with my nephew, Darius, Steve's son, who moved to Harker

Heights, TX with his family. His stepfather, Jason, was in the Army and transferred to Ft. Hood Army Base, and their family moved less than a mile away from where we lived in Killeen.

Over the next few years, I spent time getting to know Darius and his family. To have my nephew from Rosalina's side live close meant that I would have the opportunity to bond and build memories with part of my biological family. My two older children and Darius attended the same high school together, and Darius hung out with us as often as he could.

One time, I remember when I took Darius and my children to a deserted bridge in the outskirts of town in Killeen that was rumored to be haunted by a past drowning, suicide, and bus accident. We wanted to find out if the legend was true. Supposedly, you could see ghosts on the bridge.

During the drive, we were all scared, but no one wanted to admit it. The drive to the bridge was just as scary as the actual haunted bridge itself.

A ghost was supposed guarding the haunted bridge, trying to scare people away and running them off the road. We turned down an isolated dirt road that led to the bridge, and out of nowhere, a big white truck came speeding past, scaring all of us. We immediately turned around and headed back home, never making it to the bridge.

We laughed so much during the ride home, mainly because we never made it to the haunted bridge. Moments like these with Darius and my children made finding

Rosalina well worth it. Darius eventually graduated high school in 2017 and joined the U.S Army. He is currently stationed in Italy.

In 2010, I came across the Ancestry.com website that I had previously been familiar with. While searching for Rosalina, I had previously signed up for access to use their search feature for message boards but never really explored the rest of the website.

One of the website's features included creating family trees, and I decided to make a family tree for my adoptive family. I was able to trace my adoptive family's ancestors five generations back. It brought joy to my heart to share the information I discovered with my mother, who was also curious about her family lineage. This discovery made me more eager to find my birth father and learn about my ancestors.

As the years went by, the void in my heart of not knowing my birth father grew deeper. It seemed like everything reminded me that part of me was still missing; however, life happened, and searching for my birth father had to be put on hold.

Finding Myself

Reggie

"Live every day as if it were going to be your last; for one day you're sure to be right." – Harry Morant

My brother, Reggie, was hit by a car and killed instantly in Baton Rouge, Louisiana on November 2012. He had been living at a group home there for a few months.

During most of his adult life, Reggie had a struggled with mental illness and drug use. He was diagnosed as schizophrenic and bipolar, but I did not see his condition. He was just my brother to me.

Although Reggie struggled with life, his love for God never wavered. He was a devout Christian who loved the Lord, and even at his darkest times, his faith in God remained constant.

Reggie enjoyed going to church and interacting with his church family. He carried around his bible and was always ready to debate the scripture with anyone that tested it. I love to hear Reggie and my grandmother go at it about the meaning of scriptures in the bible.

I felt sad that my brother had left this world at the young age of forty-four without having the opportunity to know about his birth family. To know that his biological family would never get a chance to know him or see him hurt me deeply. I do not know if he cared to know his birth family or if he had ever talked about this with anyone, but I believe that most adoptees desire to know who they are and where they come from.

I always wondered if Reggie's mental issues stemmed from his abandonment issues. I regret that I never talked to him about being adopted. Now he was gone and would never get the chance to decide if he wanted to look for his birth family or not.

My three oldest children love their Uncle Reggie, and he loved them too. He was one of the best uncles, and he was always there for me when I needed him.

My children enjoyed spending time with Reggie, especially when he stayed overnight at our house. He would often babysit them in exchange for going to the movies to watch one of the latest Sci-Fi movies or going to his favorite restaurant.

Before his death, my mother and brother, Mike, came to visit, and we all went to visit Reggie in Baton Rouge. I hated leaving him there when we left, and I promised him he could come to visit me in Texas. I had talked to him on the phone one time, and he had asked if he come live with me, and I told him I would ask my mother, but it never happened.

I was grateful for the memories I did have with Reggie, and I wish my two youngest children would have had the chance to know him. We continued to tell our children stories about Reggie, and sometimes I still search for Reggie's birth family in North Carolina in hopes of finding someone that is looking for him. They may have the desire to find the child they had given up as baby so many years ago in 1968.

Following Reggie's death, I wondered if my brother, Mike, had a desire to find his birth family. We have never talked about him being adopted either, or with Reggie's death, I knew that I wanted to tell Mike that I would help him find his family if that's what he wanted.

Reggie's premature death helped me realize that tomorrow is never promised and that I needed to continue searching for my father no matter what.

DNA

"Be yourself, everyone else is already taken."–
Oscar Wilde

In February 2013, my daughter, Alexis, gave birth to a healthy baby boy, Khiry Zaire. Not only was Khiry our first grandchild, but he was also Alexis's first son. To know that Khiry would continue my bloodline if he decided to have children meant that future generations were dependent on my discovering my roots.

Knowing that generations would benefit from me finding my birth family made searching for my birth father that much more important. The only information I knew about my birth father was that he was in the Philippines in 1975. However, searching for someone without a name or location was difficult.

I signed up with a website called "Amerasian Children Looking for their Fathers." Some of the stories on the website were former servicemembers looking for their Amerasian children or old friends. I continued to read all the stories to see if there was a story about me. Just maybe my father had posted on this website looking for a lost child, a baby girl. I did not find anything that would make me believe he had, so I decided I would post a message looking for him:

"Posted - Hello, I am posting a message to all the soldiers who may have been at Subic Bay around the time of August 1975 when I was conceived. I am half black or Puerto Rican and Filipino and looking for my biological father. I was hoping to find anyone who may have been involved with a Filipina woman in Olongapo. At the time (August 1975) her name was Rosalina, and she was 23 or 24. She is my mother who had given me up for adoption when I was 2 in the Philippines. She is not giving me any information about my father. I was born on April 10, 1976, which would give her conception date around August 1975. I have grown up thinking I was half Black, but she has recently told me I am Puerto Rican and not Black. (Which I do not believe). If you think you may know her or were involved with her then, please contact me. Thank You!"

After reading my message, a couple of men reached out and thought I was their missing daughter. After reviewing all the information, we discovered we were not related. Knowing that there were two ladies out there whose birth fathers were looking for them gave me hope with my search.

I decided I would ask Rosalina if she had ever told my father she was pregnant with his child. Rosalina told me that she did not get the opportunity to tell my birth father she was pregnant because she never saw him again. I had so many more questions, but my questions would have to wait.

Over the next few years, I had become frustrated with my search. A lot of time had already been spent searching for a birth father, to no avail. Sometimes it was as if I was chasing a ghost. I started to lose hope that I would ever find him.

I wondered if he was still alive, and I knew if he was still alive; with each passing year, we were all getting older. Time wouldn't wait for us, and I worried that when I found him, it may be too late.

I thought about how easy it was to find my birth mother. I thought finding my birth father would be just as easy, but it seemed almost impossible without a name or location. I was ready to give up, but for some reason God would not allow me to give up.

On February 27, 2014, I decided to take the Ancestry.com DNA (deoxyribonucleic acid) test to see if it would help my search for my birth father. Just maybe he had tested too and was waiting for his child to test.

DNA is the hereditary material in humans and all other organisms. DNA is a long molecule that contains our genetic code, like a recipe book with instructions for making all the protein in our body.

When my DNA kit arrived in the mail, I was anxious and curious to discover what these results would reveal. I had so many questions about how this DNA stuff worked. I wondered if finding my birth father was as simple as taking a DNA test.

I learned that with the DNA test, I would finally see relatives that were biologically related from both sides of my birth family. However, Ancestry.com doesn't ship tests to the Philippines, so my matches from my Filipino line may be limited.

I ordered my test through Amazon.com and was excited to open the box that contained the kit. There were two small tubes, a return envelope, and instructions inside. I wondered how this little tube would give me the answers I had needed all my life. I tried to stay optimistic about the results, but I was reminded of the many brick walls I had already hit with my search.

I read the instructions several times, ensuring that I did everything correctly. I had read that people who had submitted their tests incorrectly had to retake the test several times. This was a saliva test; after spitting in the tubes, I mailed the test off and hoped for the best.

Waiting for my DNA test results to come in really tested my patience. I logged onto the Ancestry.com website several times a day, hoping that the results were in. I knew that the results would take a while to come back because the instructions stated that it might take several weeks; however, I was eager to see what the results would reveal.

Eventually, I was able to check the status of my test through a timeline on the Ancestry.com website. The timeline showed me exactly where my DNA test was in the process.

After almost two months of waiting, I logged onto Ancestry.com on April 22, 2014, and to my surprise, my DNA test results were in. I stared in amazement at the long list of my DNA matches, names, and pictures of people biologically related to me.

The results also showed the DNA breakdown of my ethnicity, which proved that I was half Black, not Puerto Rican like Rosalina had previously stated. I also had a few matches of Asian descent, which was from Rosalina's side.

I knew that my African American DNA matches were undoubtedly from my father's side of the family, and the list seemed to go on and on. Unfortunately, I did not have an instant match to a father I had hoped for. I was still grateful for the matches I had and hopeful, knowing that people on the list were a part of my father's bloodline and that someone on the list may know my father.

Seeing the list of my DNA matches was overwhelming, and I wondered if using this list to find my father would work. My strategy was to use the matches to my advantage. I knew nothing about DNA or genealogy, but I felt like this was a good start, and I was ready to learn all that I could about the process.

My closest cousin match on the list was Stephania; Ancestry.com had predicted we were second - third cousins. I was able to view a small part of Stephania's public family tree she had created on the website. I decided to send her a message and make a copy of Stephania's family tree to build it out further in hopes of finding my father within her tree.

I received my first message on Ancestry.com from John from Michigan. John explained that he was an adoptee looking for his biological parents. His story was interesting:

JenniferRose Davis

**"I am deaf. I do not knowing my biographical parents'
background at all, I were born in Bronx, New York or
Harlem, New York 1971 my mother abandoning me I
were baby foundling brown bag at station bring to
Newark, NJ ex-living with adoptive parents newborn
boy to five year old and adoptive father gave me full
John Andrew Wilson not mine, Ex-living with foster
mother five year old to 18 year old that all I know. Hope
so find matches my 1st and 2nd cousins as soon
possible... Any time call me 734-4XXX."**

Although his message was difficult to read, I
understood what John was saying; just like me, he wanted
to fill a void in his heart. I knew exactly what he was feeling,
but I didn't know how to help him.

After I replied to John's message, I decided I would
send out messages to my matches telling my story and
asking if my story sounded familiar to anyone in their
family. I thought someone would remember if their family
members were stationed in the Philippines or left a child in
the Philippines.

My original message rea. **"Hi, my name is
Jennifer, I live in Texas, and I just did my DNA with
Ancestry. I am new at all this, so you have to bear with
me. This is interesting. Anyway, I am searching for my
birth father and his side of the family, and I don't know
anything about him, not even a name or birth year. He
probably is not aware that I exist. I was told that he is
either African American or Puerto Rican. I appear to
look half Black, and my ethnicity results seem to say I
am probably half Black. I also know that I was**

102

conceived in the Philippines (Olongapo City area) and born at Subic Bay Naval Hospital. I think my birth father was possibly in the Navy or Air Force in the Philippines around 1975-1976 when I was conceived. Maybe this rings a bell regarding someone in your family. My mother is Filipino, and her name is Rosalina or Roselina. She had given me up for adoption, but I found her about 12 years ago. She's not giving me any info about my birth father. I think my birth father would be in his late 50s or early 60s. I was hoping this DNA test works and could help narrow my search down. I know this lists us as 5th-8th cousins, but I figure our connections was through my birth father and I'd give it a try. Please let me know what you think. Thanks!"

I sent this message out to what seemed like hundreds of people on Ancestry, and people responded to my message. Some shared advice and tips on searching, while others wanted access to my family tree. Some people tried asking their families about my story, but it was difficult for them to narrow it down to who it could be with little to no information about my father. I had to explain that my current family tree was a tree of my adoptive family and not my birth family.

One thing I loved about Ancestry.com is that it allowed me to connect with my blood relatives, which was something I never imaged I would do. My DNA matches, and I often communicated through messages on

Ancestry.com, but some shared their email and phone numbers. Every week, it seemed like I was calling someone or responding to someone's email. I was excited to connect with my new family members without knowing my birth father.

Reaching out to my DNA matches was not the only way I connected with my new relatives. Sometimes my matches reached out to me first. On December 30, 2015, my DNA cousin, Trina B., sent me a message through Ancestry that said, **"According to Ancestry, we are cousins. Let's see if we can make the connection."**

Trina and I exchanged phone numbers and Facebook profiles. I was excited to know that this was one of my father's cousins and somewhere down the line, we shared an ancestor. I thought Trina could help me find my father. However, I wondered if I should tell her that I was looking for my father, which sometimes scared people away.

I learned more about Trina and her family and that our connection was through her father's mother, whose last name is Pegeese/Pegues from South Carolina. I had some Pegues matches in my DNA list. We knew that were on the right track; however, narrowing it down to who was our shared ancestor would be a challenge. I shared with Trina that I was searching for my birth father, and she immediately wanted to help.

Trina played an essential role in my search. She was helpful and tried her best to help narrow down our link, but it would take some more time. Over the next few years, we exchanged many messages and shared our frustrations about our own family trees we had created.

In May 2014, I uploaded my Ancestry.com DNA results to GEDmatch.com, which allowed me to compare and analyze autosomal DNA data files from different testing companies. This website would allow us to collaborate with others who have been tested at other companies and gain access to more genetic tools to figure out how you are related to others.

I think of GEDmatch.com as a centralized place where people who have tested with different DNA agencies, such as Ancestry.com, FTDNA.com (Family Tree DNA), and 23andme.com, can compare their DNA with others. Even if you are new to learning about DNA, GEDmatch.com breaks it down for you and has tutorials to help you learn how to navigate through your DNA results.

After getting the results from uploading my DNA to GEDmatch.com, I was now staring at an even longer list of old (some matches from Ancestry.com) and new DNA matches but with attached email addresses. I was excited because although I had only tested with Ancestry.com, I could find more connections through the other sites people had tested without buying their DNA tests.

I decided I would send out one general email, just as I had done on Ancestry.com, about my story to the first few matches on the list, approximately fifty, and surprisingly, about everyone replied.

Most did a "one-on-one" comparison of my DNA with theirs before responding to my email so that they could provide me with more information about our connection. However, I received only one negative email back that read, **"We are not related, do not ever contact me again!"** Others let me down easy by saying we weren't related, but they hoped that I find what I was looking for.

Several people replied to my email offering advice on searching, even offering to help search. Each response taught me a little more about DNA and gave me more tools to use for my search.

On May 21, 2014, I received a reply from one of my emails from a former Genealogist, Greg. I told Greg my story and explained that my DNA kit number on GEDmatch.com matched his kit number. He responded, asking which kit number because he administered several kits.

After discovering my DNA did not match his kit, Greg said, **"I would like to offer you some help."** He noted that testing my DNA with Ancestry.com, the Relative Friend Finder test, was the best start because it represents the twenty-two pairs of non-sex chromosomes I inherited from my maternal and paternal lines.

Greg then explained the X and Y chromosome and how I do not have Y chromosome because I am a female. He stated that my X chromosome is the exact copy of my father's X chromosome passed between a father and sons. He explained that Ancestry.com does not offer consumers the X data, but another company called Family Tree DNA, also known as FTDNA.com, does, and it would allow me to search for matches with shared X DNA.

Greg confirmed my ethnicity and stated that my ancestral composition is 50/50, so my father was likely African American. Once again, it was confirmed that I was Black and not Puerto Rican.

Greg stated that he formerly serviced in the Marine Corps and stayed at Subic Bay in the Philippines. Greg explained how the military installation operational command worked and how I could systematically and logically determine the same unit my father was assigned based on knowing that my father was there around 1975 (when I was conceived) and when the units existed.

Greg suggested that I find out the units stationed in the Philippines during 1975. He also said that many Veterans have photos from back then on websites paying homage to their time spent in the Philippines. He advised me to search those sites, post my search requests with brief factual dates, and withhold one or two bits of information for validation for those claiming to be my father.

He also suggested that I test my DNA with a company called 23andme.com, known for phasing, which isolated matches from my maternal line. He included testing one of my children, which would also help isolate my matches.

Lastly, Greg sent me a list of naval personnel's contact information stationed at Subic Bay Naval Hospital, where I was born. He suggested that I reach out to them since they may have access to data or other persons who can get me one step closer to my father.

Greg had provided me with a wealth of information and resources to help my search. I was so grateful for his help. Although I was still learning the ins and outs of DNA, his efforts to help make the process a little easier was some of the best information I had received. I knew that his suggestions would help me get one step closer to finding my birth father.

On this same day, I got a response from a DNA match named Constance from Dallas, Texas. She said she had just compared my DNA with hers on GEDmatch.com, and we were indeed a match. She also said she compared it against her paternal grandfather, and I matched him as well. She then explained that she did not want to get me too excited but that her uncle was in the Navy and stationed in the Philippines during that time.

I spoke with Constance via telephone, and she told me I had a strong resemblance to one of her cousins. She sent a picture of her cousin, and I too was even amazed at the resemblance we had. We wondered if I could be her cousin's sister.

Constance introduced me to her family via Facebook, and they immediately welcomed me into the family. She also connected me with her uncle's children, my potential siblings, via Facebook. They were open to the idea that I may be their half-sibling, and they wanted to help.

Sadly, Constance and I realized that if we were as closely related as we thought, first cousins, our DNA would show a relation closer than distant cousins. However, I was happy that I was able to connect with new cousins.

On December 28, 2014, I sent Bill a message on Ancestry.com, regarding one of my matches. Bill explained that he had recently helped a DNA cousin find her birth parents who had abandoned her nearly fifty years ago. Little did I know that Bill would play a vital role in my search.

After sorting things out, Bill discovered that I was not a match to him but to his daughter's maternal side, a DNA kit he managed. Bill's mother-in-law, Ruth, had taken an Ancestry DNA test that he managed, and I was a match to her as well. I was excited to tell him that Ruth was one of my top DNA matches on my Ancestry.com DNA match list.

Bill had created a small part of Ruth's family tree within his family tree on Ancestry.com and gave me access to view it. I wondered if my father was listed somewhere within Ruth's tree. I decided to create a mirror tree (exact copy) of Ruth's family tree to build out and research further.

After researching Ruth's family tree out, and building it out several generations, I was excited to learn more about Ruth's ancestors, who in turn were also my ancestors. I looked for any of Ruth's relatives that were in the military in the Philippines during 1975 through the records Ancestry.com provided.

Soon after creating the new tree, I started connecting some of my DNA matches on Ruth's paternal side, the McQueen's from South Carolina. I had previously learned about another DNA match, Trina, who's family was from South Carolina, the Pegeese/Pegues.

It was amazing how my matches fit perfectly into the tree, just like a puzzle. Eventually, I would have a big picture of my birth family; however, getting to that point would take time and patience because I seemed no closer to finding my birth father.

Bill stayed in contact with me throughout my search, especially when I had questions or needed advice. He encouraged me to continue searching and to try different ways of searching. Bill sent me articles and the research he discovered on Ruth's family. He also connected me with some of my DNA matches on Facebook.

Sadly, I learned that Ruth passed away in 2016 at the age of ninety years old. I realized how blessed I was that Ruth had taken a DNA test, which had connected me to my family line. Bill said he had discussed my search with Ruth, but she could not provide any helpful information about my birth father. I was sad to know I would never get the chance to meet Ruth to tell her how significant our match to each other was to my search.

I loved that Ancestry's online membership allowed me access to millions of records. I was able to find old records for individuals that I added to my family tree dated as far back as the 1700s, including census, birth, death, marriage, voter's registration, enslaved persons, social security administration, military, transport, addresses, obituaries, and more. I also loved that I could stop and start the monthly membership as needed for my search.

What was amazing was that the records I discovered often told stories and gave me a glimpse of what life was back in those days. I could almost visualize the person's life in the records I was read.

I was able to pull up draft and military records from World War I for one of the individuals on my family tree. The records showed that he traveled by boat overseas for war in 1918, but sadly, it also showed his body returned by boat to America in 1920 due to him dying of disease.

I paused to think about the sacrifices this soldier and many others had made at such a young age. To know that these young men left their families to fight in another country for freedom, not knowing if they would ever see their families again, was heartbreaking.

Old census records always gave an abundance of information. These records helped narrow down relationships of individuals that were reported in a household. The records were only as accurate as the person providing the census information. However, I could still pull information from the record such as other household members' names, year of birth, occupation, street and home location, race, parents' birthplace, years married, literacy, education, and more. I could even link to a neighbor's census record, which sometimes told a story within itself.

Not everyone census information is available on Ancestry.com. The "72-Year Rule" protects the living, and the National Archives releases census records to the public 72 years after Census Day. As a result, the 1930 census records were released April 1, 2002, and the 1940 records were released April 2, 2012. The 1950 census records will be released in April 2022.

Access to social security and birth records was also vital to my search. These records showed the actual legal name and date of birth instead of the nickname or estimated birth dates of household members that census records and other records showed.

Some birth records were listed as delayed birth records, which meant they were not recorded at the time of birth due to the nature and time of the birth. The applicant had to provide supporting evidence of their birth date and place of birth. For example, birth certificates were not required in North Carolina until 1913.

One of my favorite records to research was obituaries. Obituaries from Ancestry.com or other online websites for African Americans only go so far back because they were not typically published in the local newspapers until the 1960s. Family members of African American families often hand-wrote about their deceased loved one's history, keeping this information in the family. Newspapers.com listed many obituaries published in the newspaper throughout the US and I was discovering a lot of individuals obituaries on my family tree.

Obituaries provided a wealth of information including names of parents, children, spouses, siblings, and other relatives. They often gave a detailed story about the individual's life, including places they lived and work or accolades they received. They usually always listed where the individuals were buried.

Obituaries also helped me connect relatives on my tree. Who best to confirm family members than someone writing an obituary? For me, finding an individual's obituary was like finding a pot of gold.

As I became more familiar with Ancestry.com and the different websites, I learned to use various tools to aid my search. I kept a little mental and sometimes physical toolbox of all the information I had discovered about DNA and genealogy.

The search for my birth father was becoming more than just a search to find him; it was becoming a love for researching genealogy, and the bonus, the prize, would be meeting my birth family and learning about my ancestors.

Life is Too Short

"Success usually comes to those who are too busy to be looking for it." - Henry David Thoreau

In November 2016, I received some devastating news from Rosalina. She explained that my sister, Jo Jo, was "dying." She said Jo Jo had a massive stroke and was currently in the hospital, brain dead. She said the family was meeting to discuss whether to take her off life support.

I had dropped to my knees and began praying, I could not believe what I was hearing. My sister, who I had become so close with over the years, was now fighting for her life.

We shared so much about our lives with each other. Jo Jo talked about her love for her two boys, Mikey and Matt. She shared how a friend's unexpected death had affected her so deeply with her willingness to continue to go on.

We talked about how she had recovered from thyroid cancer and tried to stay healthy while dealing with what life threw at her. She even talked about her separation from her husband and how that affected her. She was happy that she had found her dream job, working at a local gun shop.

During one of our last phone calls, Jo Jo asked me to come to Virginia for her 35th birthday, November 26th.We hadn't seen each other for years. I felt bad that I let so many years go by without seeing her, so I told her I would try to visit, in 2017, but she said, "no, come in November." I remember her reminding me as we got off the phone, "Come visit me for my birthday!" I told her I would try, but little did I know that only a few weeks later in November, she would be gone forever?

Jo Jo was taken off life support, and I started planning to attend her funeral in Virginia My friend, Yoshalan, attended the funeral with me to show solidarity. I was grateful she was there.

My sister's funeral service was beautiful, and it was amazing to see the love and support of her family and friends that she dearly loved. Jo Jo, even in death, was beautiful, and she looked as if she was sleeping. I kissed her goodbye and told her; I came in November.

I was happy I spent time with my brother, Steve, and his family while in Virginia. He had remarried and I was able to meet his wife, Danielle, for the first time. We shared so many laughs together and she made me feel so welcomed. I also met my beautiful niece, Summer, who I had only seen pictures of through Facebook.

I was so happy to see my youngest brother, Sam, who had grown up on me, my nephews, Jo Jo's sons, Mikey and Matt, and my sister, Maryann. Maryann gave me one of Jo Jo's beautiful pictures she had given her of sea turtles, one of Jo Jo's favorite things. She had also given me one of

Jo Jo's favorite caps. I was honored to have these keepsakes that I would cherish forever.

I was happy to see Rosalina again. She seemed more open during my visit. Rosalina even invited me to come back to visit her now that she had her own place. We talked more than we had previously, but I did not mention any questions.

I was excited for the opportunity to spend time with my family, but sad that they were under these circumstances and that my sister was not there with us. She would have been happy to know that I had come back in November.

I was grateful for the time God had granted me with my sister over the years. He knew I needed my little sister in my life. And although she was gone, she was now with Aunt Candy in heaven looking down on all of us.

After returning home from Jo Jo's funeral and having a great visit with my family, it helped put things in perspective. I decided to attempt to ask Rosalina if she could remember anything about my birth father. I felt like anything she could tell me would help my search.

I sent Rosalina a message through Facebook Messenger, this was our usual way of communicating. I told her how hard it was to search for someone with no name or information and that I hoped she could give me any information that would help me find my birth father.

Rosalina finally admitted that she did not know my birth father and she could not remember his name. She explained that she met my father by accident one night when she and a friend went out in Angeles City. Angeles

City was a city outside of Clark Air Force Base in the Philippines, a little over an hour from Olongapo City.

Rosalina could not remember anything about him. She said, "I'm sorry I can't give you any information about your father." I replied saying, "It's okay, I WILL find him!" She seemed genuinely sorry.

How could I be upset with Rosalina; I knew she was young when she met my father and it had been so many years ago. I couldn't blame her.

Her apology had given life back to my search. I was more motivated than ever to continue searching for my birth father. I jumped back into searching right away and revisited some old leads. Searching had started to become a part of everyday life for me, just as it had with my search for Rosalina.

On January 20, 2017, I sent my new DNA match, Quintin, on Ancestry.com a message about my story. Ancestry.com suggested that Quintin and I were second cousins. I felt this was a good lead because he was one of the top matches on my list.

Quintin confirmed that we are cousins per DNA, but he explained that it would be hard for him to narrow it down to who my father is without knowing a name. At that time, Quintin could not think of any of his relatives who had been in the Philippines when I was born.

Someone had suggested that I try a different route and upload my DNA results to the two other major DNA websites, FTDNA.com (Family Tree DNA) and Myheritage.com. This would yield more matches from people that may not have used Ancestry.com or uploaded to GEDmatch.com. I also bought a DNA test from 23andme.com since I could not upload my results to their site.

Once I got my DNA results from 23andme.com, I had a whole new list of matches. Names were different from the ones I had seen on the other sites, and now I had my work cut out for me. I began researching my new matches to see if I could make any connections.

Facebook had become one of my go-to search tools, which gave me a lot of helpful information about my matches along with pictures. Almost everybody had a Facebook account, or at least someone in their immediate family did, and whoever my father was, he probably had a Facebook account too.

I utilized Facebook by taking a name from the family tree or my DNA matches, searching for them on Facebook. Sometimes it an extra step of googling the person's name to get information to help search on Facebook. Often, there was a lot of information about a person's life on Facebook.

Once I found the person on Facebook, it was easy to determine who their parents, grandparents, and children were because they often posted pictures or referenced their names and tagged them in their posts. People would also post obituaries, photos of older relatives, and celebrations (birthday, wedding, birth of new baby) on their timelines. I was able to get birthdates and more, which aided in having a more accurate family tree.

Since I had not ever shared my feelings of being adopted or the progress of my search with my adopted parents, I decided to call my father and tell him about my search. This was always a sensitive subject because I did not know how he and my mother felt about searching for my birth family.

When I told my father that I was searching for my birth father, he responded, "You don't know what type of person you will find." He said this man could be in prison or be a bad person. Just from his response, I knew he was not interested in my search, and I decided not to tell him anything else about my search until I found my birth father, and hopefully prove to him he wasn't a bad person.

In the back of my mind, I knew my father was right. I never thought about my birth father being a bad person, but I also knew I had to take a chance. I would never know what type of person he was if I was afraid to find him. I knew that I couldn't be fearful of the what ifs. I had to trust that God would guide me and protect me throughout this process.

Welcome to the Philippines (Online)

"Whether you think you can or you think you can't, you're right." - Henry Ford

On February 23, 2018, Rosalina messaged me and asked me to help her find her brother in the Philippines. I was happy that she asked me to help, but what she did not know was that I had been searching for her family for years.

Previously, I was not successful in finding her family due to having limited information. I only knew Rosalina's surnames, so I befriended as many people as possible online with those last names in the Olongapo City area, hoping they were related, but I could never confirm any connections.

Rosalina finally gave me some information about her family, and I was anxious to start searching. With today's technology, I had no doubt that I would find someone in her family. She told me that her brother's name was Inocentes M. I thought, wow, what a unique name; I should have no problem finding someone with that name.

My first thought was to search for Inocentes on Facebook since Facebook had proven to be a virtual tool for searching for people. As soon as I put the name in a search, I had an instant match; Inocentes M. Jr.

I did not hesitate to send Inocentes a message that stated, I think you may be my mother's brother; my mother is Rosalina. I waited for a reply, but after I did not receive one, I thought this might be harder than I thought.

I sent Inocentes an invite to Messenger (Facebook Messenger) and tried calling him via Messenger, but there was no response. I studied his Facebook profile and noticed that he had never posted anything on his page, and he only had eight friends on his friend's list. I randomly chose one person from his list, Steven, and sent a message.

The message read, **"Hi, are you a friend of Inocentes Malaga's page? Are you related to him? I think he is my uncle. His sister, Rosalina, in the states, is looking for him.** "Shortly after, I got a response that said, **"Yes I am his grandson."**

I was happy to have found our family in the Philippines. Steven was Inocentes Jr.'s nephew and Inocentes Sr.'s great-grandson. Steven put me in touch with his mother, Catrina. Catrina was Rosalina's niece, her sister's, Rosana, daughter. Within minutes we were messaging one another.

Catrina explained that her mother, Rosana, had died on November 28, 1997, from Mayoma (ovarian cancer), and she was only forty-four years old.

Steven explained that before her death, Rosana had been looking for her sister, Rosalina, for a long time to no avail. Catrina said, **"Tita (Aunt) Rosalina left years ago and never contacted us again."** Steven said that his mother was upset with Tita Rosalina because she forgot about her family in the Philippines.

Steven told me that Rosalina and Rosana's father, Lola Inocentes, died in January 1995, but his son, their brother, Inocentes Jr., was still alive.

Catrina explained that Lolo Inocentes was a fisherman from San Roque and sometimes he didn't get a catch. She said the family struggled for money. She explained that Lolo was a sweet and kind man.

Steven also said that Rosalina's mother, Lourdes M., was still alive in the Philippines. I said, **"Wait, Rosalina's mom, Lourdes, is still alive?"** He said yes. I told him that I thought she had died, and he responded, **"No, she is still alive."**

I asked Steven if he had any pictures of his family, but he said that he had no pictures of Lourdes or Inocentes Sr. because all their photos were destroyed in a typhoon years ago. He said, **"You have many aunts on Lola Lourdes' side because she had another family."**

I would later learn that Lola Lourdes had remarried and had seven more children besides Rosalina and her other two siblings, and Lolo Inocentes Sr. had ten more children. Steven sent me pictures of his family, and I shared the news and photographs with Rosalina.

Rosalina was excited to hear that I had found her family and that her brother and mother were still alive. She said she had always thought that her mother had died when she was young and was sad to hear that her sister had passed away.

Rosalina explained that she left the Philippines in 1979 to move to the states, and she said she never talked to or saw her family in the Philippines again. It was interesting that she left the Philippines in 1979 and I left in 1978.

Over the next few days, I met all my Tita Rosana's children and most of her grandchildren online through Messenger with pictures and videos. I had also met Rosalina's brother, Tito Jhun (Inocentes Jr.), his wife, and children.

We had a three-way video call with Rosalina, her brother and me on a Messenger. This was the first time Rosalina and her brother had seen each other in almost forty years, and it broke my heart to see Tito Jhun cry during the call.

I was also able to connect with some of Rosalina's half-siblings and their children, including my Tita Aiko, who was the same age as me. Through Messenger, Tita Aiko explained that her mother, Nay (mother) Lourdes, had seven more children (Lou, Marichu, Alex, Antonio Jr., Maria Teresa, Aiko, and Ronaldo).

I also connected with my cousin Bryan, Tita Marichu's son, through Messenger, who was with Lola Lourdes at the time. He called me on video chat, and I was able to see my grandmother for the first time. It was so overwhelming that I had to take a second and gather my thoughts. I had never imagined seeing and talking to my grandmother and other relatives in the Philippines.

My grandmother (Lola), Lourdes, was eight-three years old, alive, and well. She mostly spoke Tagalog and could not understand much English, but Bryan translated for us during the call. I promised Lola I would learn Tagalog so that when I visited her in the Philippines, I could communicate with her without anyone translating for us.

After meeting the family online, we started a Facebook Messenger family group called Lourdes Apo that included most of Lola's grandchildren. Mostly, the group spoke in Tagalog, but they attempted to help me learn Tagalog by translating what they were saying into English.

I was happy to finally have a connection with my family in the Philippines. I was able to fill in my maternal the side on my family tree in Ancestry.com, and I looked forward to meeting them all in person one day.

Rosalina and I had started communicating more. We would sometimes call and talk to each other on the phone or video chat. One day, she mentioned that she was upset with seeing a post on Facebook from one of her newly found nieces in the Philippines who said something about Rosalina had never looked for them in the Philippines.

Rosalina said, **"It hurt me so much to read that post!"** She said, **"If I could turn back the times that we were separated, I would because I know it hurts and that I've done, including YOU. I regret it so much, but it is past, and there is nothing I can do now; I'm glad that we have each other now."**

This was the first time Rosalina acknowledged anything about giving me up for adoption. I replied, telling her I always wondered if she regretted giving me up, and she replied, **"Of course, I regret it from the bottom of my heart, but I just do not know what to do that time."**

Although I was glad to finally know how Rosalina felt, I had come to realize that I didn't need an explanation like I thought I did. I had forgiven her years ago, even before I had ever found her.

I was loved and wanted despite being given up for adoption. I was blessed to have been given to a wonderful family, loving adoptive parents, who did their best to raise me. I had accepted that this was the story God intended for me to have and to one day share with the world.

At that moment, I took the opportunity to ask Rosalina if she remembered anything about my father, like if he was a soldier, if he was Black or if she knew where he was from in the U.S. She responded, **"He is Black, and I didn't know his name. It was only a one-night stand; he is in the service; I don't know his name, can't remember what he looks like. It was an accident how we met. I'm sorry, I love you."** I was grateful for her response.

As I continued searching for my father, I could not help but notice that I was no closer to finding him than before. I had not had any new leads in a long time, and I started feeling hopeless and depressed, thinking that I may never find him.

I spent many days searching for him and was physically and mentally drained. Some days, I had a headache from staring at the computer screen for so long, while other days, I felt mentally exhausted from just carrying all the information and names in my head.

I felt like my efforts were in vain, and the search took up a lot of my time. It was as if I was going in circles with no real direction, and I continued to hit brick walls. I searched for years, and I was ready to give up. I needed a fresh start, new ideas, and to find the motivation again to continue searching.

As I got older, I tried to connect with my Filipino side on my own. I befriended Filipinas to learn more about the culture. I identified with being Black, but that was even questioned at times. In a bit of rage, I was once told by a family member, "You're not Black!" I was even scorned by another person for not knowing my bloodline.

My identity was always being questioned. Sometimes, I was never Black enough, or people would say I did not realize you were half Filipino; you do not look Filipino. Others would say you have a Filipino nose, or you look Mexican.

I met a Filipina lady, Jan, who I worked with in Austin, Texas. She introduced me to other Filipinos in the community and told me stories about growing up in the Philippines. She also invited me to her and her friend's gatherings and suggested that I join the Filipino Association in Austin, which held special events around the Filipino community.

I learned more about Filipino culture. I knew it was a proper gesture for Filipino elders to take their right hand,

and bring it up to touch your forehead, called mano or that meals are not considered whole unless rice is served. I did not realize that sometimes Filipinos used their hands to eat, just like my grandmother, Queen, and other Southerners had. I also learned that Black Filipinos in the Philippines endured discrimination and racism much like people of color here in the U. S. "The Indigenous people of the Philippines, known as the "Aeta" are a group related to the Negrito (Spanish term for "little Black person") ethnic group occupying parts of the Andaman Islands in India, Malaysia, and Thailand. They are characterized by their short stature, kinky hair, and dark skin."

Connections

"Family means no one gets left behind or forgotten." —David Ogden Stiers

When I was younger, I never really knew anyone else who was "adopted," except my brothers, it wasn't until I was older that I started meeting others who had been adopted.

I mostly dealt with my feelings of being adopted on my own, never talking about being adopted with my parents and never asking them questions about my adoption. It was as if I had tried to block it out.

I felt I was unloved and unwanted by my birth mother, and that was why I was given up. I wondered what was wrong with me for her to no longer want me.

I mostly held my emotions in thinking that no one would understand how I felt. As I got older, I was able to talk about being adopted more, and eventually, I was able to share my story with others.

Once I posted the progress of my search on Facebook, I realized there were others with similar experiences and circumstances like mine. It was very therapeutic for me to talk about my journey with others on Facebook.

I joined several Facebook groups related to adoptions, DNA, and genealogy. I had even found my old orphanage's Facebook page. I was able to see the orphanage I lived in; I was excited to know that that it had remained open after all these years.

I replied to a post on the orphanage's page and discovered several ladies that said they had been at the orphanage around the same time I was there or after. Some of the ladies were older than me and unlike me, could remember their experiences.

It was amazing to connect with others who were once there. I was too young to remember that time in my life; however, seeing old and current pictures did something to my soul. It was just the motivation I needed to continue searching, knowing that God never gave up on me.

Some of the Facebook groups I belonged to had members share stories about their adoption and reunion with their birth families. I read amazing stories of people who reunited with their birth families and saw these beautiful pictures of the family together again. I also read stories from people who were rejected or not accepted by their birth families once they were found.

Initially, I was happy to read these success stories, but I began feeling sad or a bit jealous about their success. I felt like how I could be happy for someone else's journey, and I couldn't even find my birth father. I felt selfish for feeling that way.

I prayed to God to change these negative feelings and guide me to my birth father. I asked God to give me a clue that I was searching in the right direction. I believed that I would someday be able to share my story, just as others had done. Eventually, my time would come, and I had to be patient for **God's Perfect Timing**.

On December 13, 2017, I "waved" at Natosha in Facebook Messenger, who was half Filipino and half Black. I had just seen her Facebook post of meeting her birth father and four half-sisters for the first time in New York. A television station had aired her story. I was so excited after watching her video, and I knew I wanted to reach to congratulate her.

Natosha waved back, and our friendship began. We discovered that we had a lot in common, and we were so amazed at how our stories were so similar. She was born in the Philippines, adopted by a Black military family, and brought to the states.

Natosha explained that she had always thought her father was her biological father until she took a 23andme DNA test and discovered her true biological father. She stated that she was never looking for her birth father; she just happened to find him when she did the test to find out her ethnicity. She said that her biological father knew about her but never knew she had been given up for adoption.

Natosha went on to say that when she initially did the DNA test, a DNA cousin match reached out to her, but she thought the cousin knew her birth mother who is Filipina. However, as soon as she told the DNA cousin that she was from the Philippines, the cousin knew her father because his family had always known he had left a child in the Philippines.

Over the next few days, Natosha and I shared a lot about our lives with each other. We talked about growing up, our adoption struggles, and our adoptive families. We both related with growing up in our adoptive homes and how our families did not encourage us to learn about our Filipino heritage. Natosha also had two adopted older brothers and she was the youngest, just like me.

It felt good to find someone who could relate to things I had gone through or what I was feeling. Natosha was so easy to talk with. We connected because of our similar life stories which were so much alike on many different levels.

Natosha gave me some insight into what it was like meeting her biological father and siblings. She explained how happy and accepting they were of her.

Unfortunately, Natosha's adoptive parents had already passed away, and they never knew she connected with her birth father. She had also never known her birth mother.

God had put Natosha in my life at just the right time to show me what was waiting for me and to remind me to keep the faith. Natosha's story motivated me to continue with my search despite the brick walls or setbacks.

Shortly after learning about Natosha's story, I was reading another Facebook group's timeline, and a post caught my attention that read: "Breaking News- Update, Sibling Found. God is good!" Once again, I was drawn to read the story and fascinated by the details that sounded like mine.

132

Terrence, who was searching for his sibling from the Philippines, an adoptee who was half Filipino and half Black, had just posted he had found his sister. I had seen Terrence's previous posts about searching on the group's timeline and was excited to know that his sibling, Naaja, had been found in Texas. I congratulated Terrence, and he replied, **"You're next, Jennifer!"**

Terrance explained that if it were not for the fact that his father's two nephews had done their DNA with 23andme.com, they might still be looking for his sister because she had not done a test with Ancestry.com; she had done one with 23andme.com.

Terrance explained how Facebook and Facebook Messenger were vital to his search for his sister. He talked about how he and his family never knew if their sister existed, and at times, it felt like he was chasing an urban legend.

Terrence was the first to introduce me to two websites, zabasearch.com and truepeoplesearch.com, and he explained that these sites would list relatives in the home or other people who lived with them. He suggested that I make myself a "little chart" and utilize the DNA tools from the different websites. He also suggested I watch YouTube videos regarding searching.

Over the next few months, Terrance and I got to know each other. As I told him more about my story, I became his "unofficial adopted sister." When Terrence first saw my posts on Facebook about my search, he thought I could be his sister. However, after researching a little more, he realized I was too young to be his sister.

Terrance insisted that I looked like Rosalina and jokingly said, **"Y'all favor, I need to see your Daddy though."** I replied, **"LMAO (Laughing my ass off), me too!"** I usually get that response after people saw a picture of Rosalina, but I, too, wondered what my resemblance to my father was.

Although Terrence was planning to meet his newly found sister, he continued to help with my search. He dove in headfirst and spent a lot of time sorting through names and matches. Terrance helped me navigate through my family tree and my matches I found on Facebook. He was always available when I needed him, especially when I needed a virtual shoulder to cry on.

Terrance insisted that we look into my DNA match, Quintin, from Ancestry.com. He felt that this was a good lead to finding my father and he thought the connection was through Quintin's mother's paternal line, the McCreary/McCary's. Terrance messaged twenty people on Facebook with the last name McCary through Messenger, hoping to find the McCary relative related to Quintin.

Shortly after, I received a message from Michelle, who explained that she received a message from Terrance regarding her family, the McCary's. She explained that her "granddad Jack" was Quintin's grandfather, Abe's nephew, but he had died in the 1990s when she was still in high school.

Michelle stated that she did have uncles, but she was not aware of any uncles who were in the military around the potential age I had suggested my father would be. She stated that she wanted to help research this more, and she would let me know if she found out anything else.

Terrence's sense of humor and positive energy always picked my spirits up when I felt hopeless with my search. His humor was the medicine I needed that gave me the strength to go on. He encouraged me to be patient and reminded me that life is short. He told me, **"You're next. Keep the faith! Your day is right around the corner!"**

Terrance explained that since finding his sister, his passion was to start an organization that helps Blasians (individuals of Black and Asian descent) from other countries with similar stories like mine and Naaja's. He hopes to provide comfort and support and is eager to learn and understand more to help Blasians throughout their journey of searching for their families.

Terrance invited me to a small Facebook Messenger group called DNA experts. This group consisted of a small group of people who loved to research genealogy. Terrence introduced me to Sandra from the group, who was knowledgeable in DNA and genealogy and willing to help.

He also introduced me to Diane in the group, a Filipina currently living in Olongapo City, Philippines, who had helped Terrance find his sister. Diana offered to help me in any way she could from the Philippines.

Diane introduced me to my first search angel, Sue, who had helped her find her ex-boyfriend's father. I had heard about search angels from some of the Facebook groups I belonged.

A search angel is a person who volunteers their time, energy, and support to help someone find their family. Most search angels have been through searches and reunions themselves, and this is their way of "giving back" or paying it forward to people that have helped them.

I reached out to Sue in a private message and asked for her help with my search. She responded immediately and asked to view my family tree on Ancestry. I was excited at the thought that this may work and that I had a fresh new set of eyes looking at my DNA. At this point, I was ready to try anything.

Sue stated, **"There is always a chance you will find who you are looking for but know that you may not right away."** She wanted me to understand that she was not giving me false, fast hope with this method and that it sometimes takes a long time to find who you are looking for.

Sue explained that she had been helping two other individuals searching for their families for about a year. However, she still could not figure out their biological relative because of a NPE (non-parental event), meaning someone had a child they did not know about until they got that "magical DNA match."

Sue had not known that I had been searching for years, so waiting was not going to be an issue for me. I was in it for the long haul. I had hit several brick walls along the way, and I understood that things do not just happen overnight. I was just grateful that she was willing to offer her time, in addition to the two other people she was already helping. I tried to thank Sue as often as I could, but she would always reply, **"No thanks needed..."**

As Sue looked at my DNA, she zeroed in on my DNA match, Quintin, and made a mirror tree of Quintin's tree, building out his family lines. Sue told me that she believed that Quintin's grandmother or grandfather was the sibling of my unknown great-grandmother or grandfather, but the question was, which side of Quintin's family.

We began studying both sides of his family, hoping to determine which side I was related to; however, it seemed like I had DNA matches from both of Quintin's family lines. I had three DNA matches connected to the Mims' and a McCary match. Sue explained that it was not uncommon for individuals to be related to both sides because first cousin marriages were common back then.

Sue also explained that the way she searches is once she creates a mirror tree, she attaches the person's DNA to the tree, and Ancestry.com will generate SAH's, shared ancestor hint, and from there, she looks at that family's line for a birth relative. She explained that matches must already have a family tree created to get a SAH match.

I had not learned much about the SAHs on Ancestry.com, but I often saw SAHs pop up on my family tree I had created. I just did not know how to use them to my advantage. I was excited to learn this new tool and incorporate into my search.

Sue stated that she thought my connection was through Quintin's mother's paternal line, the McCary's; this was the same news I had received from Terrance. I felt like we were on the right track.

Sue created a mirror tree called "helping Jennifer" of Quintin's family tree and invited me to use the tree on Ancestry.com. I started building out this tree in all directions, being sure to document any records that showed someone who had been in the military in the Philippines.

Over the next few months, Sue and I exchanged messages about the search. Like others that helped me search, Sue was always there if I had a question or needed her to look at something I had discovered. She shared her wealth of knowledge and helped me learn the twists and turns of DNA and genealogy.

I decided to look more into Quintin's mother's maternal like the Mims' side of his family. Not knowing which side of Quintin's family, I was related to, I figured it wouldn't hurt to look at both lines.

I had even called to talk to one of the oldest living Mims, Ms. Novella, who was ninety-three years old in Alabama. Ms. Novella's son, who I had reached out to first, said his mother had one of the sharpest memories of anyone he knew at that age, and he suggested I give her a call.

I called and talked to Ms. Novella and realized he was right; she remembered a lot of her family's history. She told me that she only knew of one close relative, her grandson, who was in the military, but he had not been to the Philippines.

I decided to explore my McCary DNA match, V McCary from Florida, from Quintin's mother's paternal line. I located this match on Facebook and determined his mother, father, and grandparent's names from the photos he posted on his timeline. I tried reaching out to the McCary match several times through Ancestry.com messages and Facebook Messenger, but I never got a response.

Quintin's maternal grandfather, Abe McCary, was born in Evergreen, Alabama. I remember hearing about Evergreen, Alabama, because my first DNA match's, Stephania, maternal family was from Evergreen.

Abe later moved to Pensacola, Florida, and then relocated to Johnstown, Pennsylvania, where he started a family. Abe was one of two men who was tragically killed in an explosion at his job during the Johnstown Flood of 1977, known as the second great flood of Johnstown, PA. I had found this information on Newpapers.com.

In May 2018, I received a notice in my email of a new DNA match on Ancestry.com named Quintella, and I did not hesitate to reach out to her. I sent her my famous message about my adoption story, and she responded right away, asking me to call her.

Quintella was so happy to hear from me and was opened to sharing information about her family. She suggested that I email a mutual DNA match of ours, who she had recently been in touch with, Di Shawn, and ask for help. I emailed Di Shawn right away and shared my story. He responded quickly.

Di Shawn and his father were listed as my cousins on both Ancestry.com and Gedmatch.com. Being a DNA match to Di Shawn's father made it easy for him to know that our connection was through his paternal side; however, he needed more information to dig further to find the link to our common ancestor.

Di Shawn indicated that he thought our connection was through the Gilmore's since I was related to him and Quinella, and they both were related to the Gilmore's. He shared his phone number with me to talk more about my search.

Over the next few months, Di Shawn continuously helped me throughout my search. He was the first person who introduced me to fold3.com, a military records search. This was a great resource that listed individuals' military service and more. Most websites like these offered a free trial period, which allowed me to search their site for free before buying a subscription.

Di Shawn also welcomed me into his family with open arms. He was always there to help me in any way he could. He always responded when I texted or called him, even late at night. He was often up late researching his genealogy.

Di Shawn would often send me leads and pictures of family, and I would forward him the latest information I had found about my search. He studied both of our family trees, looking for the missing link. Di Shawn was determined to find our connection. He celebrated our little victories of getting closer to finding my father, and he always encouraged me not to give up even after I had setbacks.

Di Shawn had become my "go-to" person when it came to my search. He was knowledgeable and had his way of researching. He never seemed discouraged, even after we had gone down a wrong lead.

At one time, we thought that one of his relatives, James, a servicemember who was stationed in the Philippines in 1975, was my father. We spent a lot of time looking at James' pictures and records to determine if James was my father. I had even sent Rosalina a picture of James, but she said no.

We located James' younger brother, Terrance, in Texas on Facebook, and I called and talked to him on the phone. We learned that James and his daughter, my potential half-sister, Debra, had already passed away. Terrance was opened to helping me and suggested that I connect with James' son-in-law, Sherrod, who would be willing to talk to me.

Sherrod thought there was a good chance that I could be his wife's sister. Sherrod was excited to know that I could be his son's aunt, and he was ready to introduce me to his son. I thought it was best to wait until we had confirmation, but I was just as excited to know that I might have a new nephew. I asked Sherrod if he would be willing to allow his son to do a DNA test if needed, and he said yes.

Di Shawn and I eventually learned that James could not be my father. It was hard for me to tell Sherrod that I was not related to his son. I was grateful that he was willing to help, and I had hoped that we were related. Sherrod understood and wished me the best with my search.

Despite all efforts and the disappointment of knowing we had the wrong potential father, Di Shawn and I switched gears and continued with the search. He encouraged me not to worry and assured me that we would find my father. His support for my journey was constant and undeniably one of the reasons I could not give up now.

As I continued building my tree, I connected with Quintin on Facebook Messenger again. I kept noticing this last name kept coming up in my search and that he had people on his Facebook friend's list with the same last name.

I decided to explore this surname a little more. I chose someone with the last name from Quintin's friend's list and sent them a message through messenger. I crossed my fingers and hoped they would be willing to respond to a stranger.

I waited for Derrick to respond to my message, and he was willing to help. He responded with his mother's maiden name, McCary, and that he and Quintin's mother were sisters. The name McCary had seemed to come up a lot in my search.

Derrick tried to think of any close relatives who had been in the military stationed in the Philippines, but he could not think of anyone. He suggested that I talk to his sister, Michelle S., who lived with their mother, who he thought could provide me with more information.

I reached out to Michelle S. on Facebook Messenger. She was intrigued by my story and stated that she has a big family. She said that she would ask her mother, Pauline, and others about my story, but she did not think she had any family members in the Philippines that could be my father.

I sent Michelle S. pictures of me, and her response was, **"My mom said you have our nose,"** I thought, my Filipino nose? It was interesting to hear that my nose came from my birth father's side and not from my Filipino side.

Michelle S. provided me with some information about her grandfather, Abe McCary. We had already found Abe's obituary online, and Michelle suggested that I look up the name Johnnie McCary, her mother's half-brother. She also stated that after talking to her mother, her mother said that her father's brothers were Al, Son, and Jim, and that they all lived in Evergreen, Alabama and that he also had two sisters.

Michelle S. and I continued to stay in touch. I continued to update her on my progress. She was always willing to ask her mother questions for me. Her mother tried to help by remembering things about her family from the past. I was grateful for Derrick, Michelle S., and their mother's willingness to help a stranger, especially someone asking questions about their family.

I was grateful for the information Michelle S. shared with me and little did I know, the name Johnny McCary would come up again. However, Johnny's last name was Harris, not McCary, because he carried his mother's last name and not his father, Abe's last name. I researched more information about Johnny Harris and discovered his obituary online.

Johnnie Harris, Quintin's half great uncle, was born in 1930 in Evergreen, Alabama and had grown up in Pensacola, Florida, He relocated to Cincinnati, Ohio, with his wife and young children. He eventually had six children with his wife, Mabel. Johnnie died in 2014 in Cincinnati.

I was sad to learn that Johnnie had already passed away. I knew this meant that I would never get to meet him if he were related to me. I always worried that my search would lead to relatives I missed meeting by a few years due to them passing away.

Around June of 2018, I reached out to Greg, the Genealogist who had helped me in the past. Greg and I had email contact back in 2014 after receiving my DNA results. And he provided me with information that would help with my search.

Greg had previously determined the relationship of his great-grandparent through DNA, and he was willing to help me with my search again. I had hoped that he could use his expertise to narrow down my search now that I had leads and was further in my search.

Greg remembered me from my 2014 email. He reviewed my DNA on GEDmatch.com. After answering a few questions, updating him on my discoveries, and reminding him of my case, Greg suggested that he thought one of the top DNA matches, Stephania, and I shared either a grandfather or great grandfather.

Greg was primarily interested in how much DNA I shared with my other matches than my family tree. He tried to explain the process to me, stating that this helped identify a common ancestor. He analyzed the chromosomes shared

144

with my matches across DNA segments, a skill that I am still trying to perfect.

Greg suggested that I test my 24 years old son, at the time, with another company other than Ancestry.com. He explained that this gets my son's DNA out there (and by default, half of me) to those who have tested with 23andme and have not uploaded it to GEDmatch.com.

He also explained that 23andme automatically phases the DNA and paints each chromosome (all segments of DNA that differ) with admixture. Phasing is a technique of identifying which DNA came from your mother and your father.

Next, Greg took the time to teach me the step-by-step process of triangulating, a process that looks for matches across all chromosomes. He also introduced me to the Philippines Amerasian Research Center in Angeles City, Philippines, Pearl S. Buck Foundation, and the Philippines American Guardian Association, Inc. (PAGA), excellent resources for my search. He wished me luck on my search, and I thanked him for his help.

I decided to revisit one of my top matches, Jeremy, from 23andme.com, who I had researched before. I had sent Jeremy, who is biracial, some messages, but he never responded.

Jeremy's father was African American and is most likely the person that I was related to. I discovered who his parents were by searching Facebook. I also saw a picture of his grandmother, Ms. Evelyn, a Minister, who he had written a post about. I decided I would reach out to her.

145

To my amazement, after researching my family tree, I already had Jeremy's grandparents, Edward, and Evelyn, on my family tree. His grandfather was closely related to one of my top DNA matches, Ruth. I sent Ms. Evelyn a message on Facebook Messenger and hoped she would respond.

Reaching out to strangers on Messenger and Facebook was easy but getting them to respond to a stranger asking questions about their family was hard. Some people are not opened to answering messages from people they do not know or even sharing information about their family online.

When sending a message, I always started by telling my story first, hoping that the person would at least hear my story and then decide if they would like to respond to my message or not. I understand why someone would not respond to a stranger's message.

Thankfully, Ms. Evelyn responded to my message. I sent her screenshots of her grandson's DNA match to me, and of her and her husband's place on the family tree, which included her husband's relatives, the McQueen's. I shared with her that I was also a DNA match to Ruth, who passed away.

Ms. Evelyn confirmed that her husband's family are the McQueen's from South Carolina. She informed me that the McQueen's were having an upcoming family reunion in Cheraw, South Carolina, this year, and she suggested I attend. She provided me with the date of the reunion just in case I wanted to attend the reunion. I was honored that she asked me to attend the reunion.

Ms. Evelyn then asked me to call her. I was happy that she wanted to talk on the phone; it was often hard to explain what I wanted to say in a message.

During the phone call, Ms. Evelyn suggested reaching out to Ms. Gladys. She had recently met Ms. Gladys and three other McQueen family members, while trying to learn more about her husband's side of the family.

She explained that two of the McQueen ladies, including Ms. Gladys, were the oldest living McQueen's, and they may be able to help with my search. Ms. Evelyn stated her meeting the McQueen ladies must have been God putting things in place for me. I was thankful for Ms. Evelyn giving me information regarding the McQueen's and was excited to call and speak with them.

I called Ms. Gladys, who was willing to talk to me. She told me that she was the oldest living McQueen, and her grandfather was Sky McQueen. I immediately recognized Sky McQueen's name as one of the ancestors already listed on the family tree I had created of Ruth's family, and I knew that Sky McQueen was Ruth's grandfather.

I explained to Ms. Gladys that Ruth was one of my top matches on Ancestry.com. She stated that Ruth was her older sister who passed away. She tried to think if any of her family members in the service had that been to the Philippines but could not think of anyone. Ms. Gladys said she knew of a couple of close relatives in the service, but not necessarily in the Philippines. She stated that she would continue researching my story and asked some other family members to see if they could figure this out.

Before our conversation ended, Ms. Gladys invited me to the McQueen Family Reunion in Cheraw, South Carolina, the same reunion Ms. Evelyn had mentioned. To be invited to a reunion where there would be family related to me was everything I ever wanted. I told her I would think about coming to the reunion. However, I thought it was too soon to attend the reunion, especially since I had not found my father yet, and wouldn't be able to explain my relationship to everyone.

Over the next few months, I stayed in contact with Ms. Gladys and Ms. Evelyn and updated them on the progress of my search. Ms. Gladys talked about her daughter, Theresa, who I had already been in communication with since Theresa was one of my Ancestry.com DNA matches.

I explained to Ms. Gladys that I had talked with Theresa months before ever meeting her (Ms. Gladys), and she had invited me to meet her and her daughter when she was living in Anaheim, California. I thought it was interesting how the connection with Theresa tied back to Ms. Gladys.

Ms. Gladys continued to invite me to the family reunion in August. I thought it was nice of her to include me, but I was not ready to attend the reunion just yet. Later, I realized that I should have taken her up on the offer.

As I continued searching for my birth father, I would update my mother on my search. She knew I was searching and had heard me talking about it here and there, but I never spoke with her about my progress.

My mother explained she had a friend, Donna, who loved genealogy and would be willing to help me. She called Donna, who invited us over to her home. I was excited for a fresh pair of eyes to look at my research.

After arriving at Donna's home, I told her my story, just as I had done many times before. She pulled up some information on her computer and explained how she searched for individuals. She shared tips and viewed my DNA on Ancestry.com. We exchanged phone numbers, and she promised to let me know if she found anything promising.

Around July 2018, I reached out to Sandra from the DNA Experts Facebook group that Terrence had invited me to. I asked her for a fresh pair of eyes to look at my research and she was willing to help.

Sandra decided we should talk on the phone instead of through Messenger; she said she would rather hear an "oral history" on what I knew so far. We exchanged phone numbers, and I immediately called her.

Sandra suggested I view a list of Navy decommissioned ships in the Philippines during the timeframe around my birth. This was also what Greg, the Genealogist, had previously suggested I do.

Sandra also sent me websites and Wikipedia links regarding a Subic Bay Naval Base, Ship BRP Rajah Lakandula (PF-4), commissioned into the Philippines on July 27, 1976. She explained that she liked to review history first to help her understand the adoption process. I forwarded her a YouTube video of the Philippines regarding Olongapo City.

She then informed me of my maternal DNA matches on Ancestry.com; they were my non-African American matches. She also asked for a list of surnames from my maternal side. I only knew of Nivero (Lola Lourdes's maiden name), Malaga, and Avellano.

Sandra discovered that one of my third cousin DNA matches, Rico, on Ancesty.com was also a distance cousin match to her. She went on to say that when she viewed my DNA matches on Ancestry.com, she discovered that my close matches' surnames were Mallory, Gandy, and McQueen and that I had several Burgess's matches. She also mentioned that Williams's surname was prominent with my fourth cousin matches on my list and, Campbell's. She suggested that individuals with the last names Mallory, Mims' and Gandy be my priority research.

Sandra was the first to introduce me to DNA Detectives, a Facebook group with over 130 million members started by CeCe Moore, a Genetic Genealogist.

The group focused on using DNA to help the biological family for adoptees, foundlings, donor-conceived individuals, unknown paternity, and other types of unknown parentage cases. I joined the group and was excited about the enormous support and information available. Sandra encouraged me to post my story within the group, which I did.

I shared with Sandra that I posted my story in the DNA Detectives group and two other Facebook groups, I was stationed at Subic Bay, and I was stationed at Clark Air Force Base. Clark Air Force Base was in the Philippines, close to where I was born, Subic Bay. There were servicemembers within the groups that were stationed at both places. I thought, surely, my father was a part of one of these groups and would recognize my story.

What I love about the Facebook groups is that I can connect with others by writing on their post or sending them a private message. A lot of the questions I had regarding DNA and genealogy had already been asked by group members, and I only had to search the topic using the search tool within the groups. I could also choose to post my questions within the groups.

Sandra also suggested that I send letters to organizations willing to help with my search. She stated that agencies would help me at no cost, but I had to have already done most of the work. She asked if I had registered with Adoption Reunion Registry Records, and I told her I had not. She also told me to consider hiring a private investigator to help me find my father, but I would have to pay money for the service.

Sandra continued to look at my DNA makeup that I had downloaded onto GEDmatch.com. She included that I was a strong match to one of my Ancestry.com DNA matches, Stephania, and that we most likely shared a great grandparent on the paternal side. I was excited to hear this because I had recently reached out to Stephania, and she informed me that she was looking for her biological father.

JenniferRose Davis

Over the next few weeks, Sandra continued to help me with my search. She had some great ideas and resources that she shared with me, and I was grateful for her help.

I had been so wrapped up in my search that I did not realize that Sandra was dealing with her own issues. I felt bad. She shared that this past month had been rough for her, but with God's grace she was getting through it. I appreciated her willingness to continue to help me.

Search Angels

"Spread love everywhere you go. Let no one ever come to you without leaving happier." -Mother Teresa

On August 18, 2018, Venies from Germany reached out to me through Facebook after responding to one of my posts in a DNA Facebook group.

Venies stated that if I needed help, she was willing to look at my DNA. Once again, I was grateful for the offer, and I usually never turn down anyone who offered to help with my search.

I invited Venies to look at my DNA results and family tree on Ancestry.com. Venies explained that she felt the best way to start a search was to review the individual's DNA matches. She decided to create her mirror family tree of me on Ancestry.com because she had her own way of searching that she found helpful in the past.

Venies went on to explained that she looks for common ancestors that match the individual. She uses a picture of an arrow for the individual's profile to indicate their connection or family line on the family tree.

She believed one of my top matches was Quintin's mother's maternal line, the Mims, who were a common ancestor for us. I explained that we had researched the Mims', but I matched both sides of his family.

Venies asked if I had connected with my two top DNA matches, Quintin and Stephania. I told her that I had reached out to both, and they seemed to want to help but could not provide much information regarding their family without the name or location of my birth father. She also asked if I had spoken to my DNA match named Samantha H, but I told her I was not familiar with that match, and I would have to research more information regarding Samantha.

I explained that Quintin has a small family tree on Ancestry.com with both sides of his family, but we could not narrow down which side of Quintin's family line my birth father was from.

Venies stated that she had not found any connections to me from the McCary side, Quintin's mother's paternal line, only from his mother's maternal line, the Mims' side. I told her that I had a McCary DNA match from Florida in my list of DNA matches, but the person's family tree on Ancestry.com was private, so I could not view it.

Venies and I decided to research the McCary match a little more, but we could not determine either way. I was able to find my McCary DNA match on Facebook but was hesitant about sending him another message because he never responded to my first message. I decided not to send a message.

Venies was starting to feel that my connection might be from both sides of Quintin's' family lines, the McCary's and the Mims' side, which is what my search Angel Sue had previously mentioned. I noticed that Quintin was coming up a lot in our research, and I felt he might be the link to my birth father.

Venies had several ideas regarding searching, and she mentioned that she had a contact at the National Archives, and they could help me with records. She suggested that I ask the contact to find a Black soldier in the Philippines, Olongapo, around 1975 or 1976, with the surname Mims born no later than 1958.

I never followed up on this lead, and over the next few months, Venies and I went back and forth with our research of the Mims and McCary family lines.

We laughed because we had searched so much that she jokingly stated she was cross-eyed from staring at the computer screen. She needed a break from searching, and I did too, but I could not stop searching. I knew that if I stopped, it would be missed time I could never get back of knowing my birth father.

As Venies began to dig deeper into the family tree, she kept me updated on the latest information she discovered. I was amazed at her efforts to update and maintain the family tree she created on Ancestry.com.

I decided to use her tree as my master tree, and just like my previous search angels, I tried to thank her many times, but she stated, **"No need to thank me, I had my**

search angels. Now I see it's my turn to help, and I hope to find your dad."

On August 21, 2018, I received a Facebook message from one of the sweetest women I would ever meet, LaDona, a search angel from Virginia. LaDona reached out to me after reading one of my posts in the Facebook regarding searching for my father.

LaDona's commitment and willingness to help me with my search, a stranger, is what stood out about her. She expressed that it made her heart feel happy to help others, and if I would like her help, she was available. I was excited to have her join my search team; the more eyes I had looking at the information, the greater the chance of finding my father.

LaDona explained that she had found her paternal grandfather about four years ago, and since then, she had successfully helped others connect to their birth family. Not only was she helping me, but she was also assisting another adoptee in finding his parents as well. She kept me updated with the latest information she discovered and was always a phone call away if I needed her.

I shared my DNA information on Ancestry.com and other sites with LaDona. She asked about one of my matches, Samantha. Samantha's name had come up often, and I had yet to follow up on this lead. She studied the shared matches I had in common with Samantha and was interested in learning more about my DNA matches, Quintin, Stephania, and Samantha.

LaDona also added my information to her "Becky" family tree, one combined tree she used for all the people

156

she was helping. She also studied several trees from different family lines trying to find a link. She had access to various other resources that helped with the search. She was able to pull information that listed more details than I could access.

Initially, LaDona did not think my father was from the Mims' family line, and she focused on the McCary family line. She had a lot of questions about A B or Abe McCary's family, Quintin's maternal grandfather.

LaDona found an obituary for Abe McCary, which had a lot of helpful information in it. She wondered why Abe's mother's name was listed as Elizabeth in an Ancestry.com census record, but his obituary listed his mother as Hattie. She also wondered why the census record did not list Abe as living with the rest of the McCary's at seven years old and if Abe's father had two families or if they all intermixed.

At first, LaDona started as my just search angel, but she quickly became a dear friend. We shared laughs and cries through the short time I had known her. She told me that her best friend is a first-generation Pinoy-American, and her Godson is mixed, Euro-American.

LaDona often shared a glimpse of her life with me, she was enjoying life to the fullest. She would often tell me about her fishing outings and family gatherings. She even invited me to visit her in Virginia Beach the next time I visited Rosalina, and I looked forward to taking her up on her offer one day.

She also shared with me that one of the most challenging times in her life was when a family member was a victim of a recent mass shooting. Although this was a trying time in her life, she never stopped helping me with my search. She was there with me until the end.

Around October 2018, my other search angel, Venies, pinpointed my connection was through the McCary family line and not the Mims'. She felt that a common ancestor with the last name McQueen was the missing link. I thought of Ruth, one of my close DNA matches; her maiden name was McQueen. We had previously explored this before. I had forgotten to tell Venies of my DNA match with Ruth. We added Ruth to the family tree Venies was working on and built her line out further, hoping to find someone that married a McCary.

I started feeling that we were on the right track and so close to finding my father. I felt it in my heart, and I knew God was guiding me straight to him. With everyone helping me search, family, DNA cousins, and search angles, one of us would surely find the missing link. We all agreed that my connection was through the McCary's and McQueen's.

Around November 2018, I decided to reach out to Quintin to let him know what we had discovered. Ancestry.com listed Quintin and me as second cousins, but we knew that Ancestry.com was a little off with relationships which meant we were closer than second cousins, more like first cousins once removed.

I had never heard of the term "once removed" until I began searching. A cousin once removed means they are from the generation immediately above or below you. So, your first cousin's child or your parent's first cousin is your first cousin once removed. And your second's cousin child or parent's second cousin is your second cousin once removed and so on.

I knew that my father would be closely related to Quintin, most likely his first cousin. This meant that Quintin could be my first cousin once removed.

I initially reached out to Quintin 2017, he could not provide much help without a name or location; however, he tried to help as much as he could. I updated Quintin on my progress. I explained that I had some Mims's DNA matches, but I also discovered a DNA match from his mother's paternal line, the McCary's.

Quintin stated he was getting confused about which side of his family I was related to him since I initially told him the Mims' side, and now, I thought it was the McCary side. He stated that he had a couple of cousins in the service overseas from the McCary side and that he would reach out to them and let me know what he found out. He also connected me with his mother, Ms. Deloris, to try and see if she could help sort things out.

I was excited to call Quintin's mother, Ms. Dolores, who was so sweet and willing to help. Ms. Delores and Pauline, Michelle's mother, are sisters. Ms. Deloris explained that her mother passed away when she was young and she was raised by her grandparents, the Mims.

Ms. Deloris and I talked about her aunts and uncles from her mother's maternal side; I learned about the people she mentioned through the family tree I had created. However. Ms. Deloris was still clueless about who she thought my father might be from Mims' side.

After speaking with Ms. Delores, I decided to revisit the McCary family line to see if anything stood out. Now that I was more familiar with both sides of Quintin's family, I would notice if anything did stand out.

Around the same time Quintin talked to me about his cousins who had been in the service, LaDona zeroed on Melvin. He was Quintin's first cousin from his mother's paternal side, the McCary's. LaDona found an obituary of Melvin's father, Johnnie Harris., the obituary we had previously seen. I read it again with sadness.

Johnnie had died in 2014, and if Melvin was indeed my father, I had missed the opportunity of meeting my grandfather by a few years. He would never know about me, and I would never get to meet him.

Needle in a Haystack

"Winning isn't everything but wanting to win is." -Vince Lombardi

B rick walls are an understatement when researching genealogy. I had hit so many brick walls along the way, that I was ready to give up. However, God would not allow me to give up.

To my surprise, Quintin's mother, Ms. Deloris, had just taken an Ancestry.com DNA test, and she showed up as my top DNA match on my list. The puzzle pieces started to fit together perfectly.

We reviewed the shared centimorgans, DNA, between Ms. Deloris and me. We shared 442 CMS (centimorgans). I used the DNA Painter tool to help estimate our relationship, which suggested that she was a half great Aunt.

I decided to search Melvin's name on a website called truepeoplesearch.com. LaDona used another resource to pull more information about him; all his information was there, such as his: age, address, phone number, email, and relatives that were currently or previously associated with him. It was crazy to find so much information about a person on the internet.

From the information we found, it appeared that Melvin's mother, Mabel, was still living and I remember her name from reading Johnnie Harris obituary. Mabel was in her eighties, and I had not found a death record, obituary, or any information online that indicated she had passed away. I was excited to know that if Melvin was my birth father, I had a grandmother that was still living as well.

I continued to add records to the McCary side of the family tree we had created, focusing more on Melvin. I stopped in my tracks as I uncovered a military record of Melvin's that listed his military service in the Philippines in 1975.

Could Melvin be my birth father? Could this be him? I thought, how likely was this person, Melvin, around the same age/generation that my father would be and that he served in the military in the Philippines in 1975? I considered this a significant lead and that we had probably solved the puzzle.

I asked Quintin about his cousin, Melvin, and he said Melvin had been in the service in the Philippines but that he thought that I was related to him through his mother's maternal side, the Mims'. I told Quintin that I had matches on both sides of his family so that the possibility could be on either side.

I was overwhelmed at the thought we had possibly found my birth father. All the years of searching and all the research we had done to get to this point, the hundreds of emails I had sent and the people I met along the well, it had all come down to this very moment; the moment I believe we had just found my birth father.

I wasted no time searching for Melvin on Quintin's Facebook friend list, and there he was, but he had more than one profile. I looked through his profiles, trying to learn more about him. He didn't post much information, but seeing his pictures shocked me.

Although I did not look exactly like him, I saw similar features, especially in my children. His nose was the first thing I noticed, just like mine, but not my Filipino nose I thought I had always had. It was a mixture of both.

My emotions ran high as I shared Melvin's picture with my search angels, family, and friends. I waited for responses to hear what everyone thought. Some people thought I looked like him, while others said it was hard to tell because I look so much like Rosalina.

I began comparing Melvin's pictures to pictures of my children to see if anyone thought there was a resemblance. I created a side-by-side image of Melvin and my oldest son, Carliss, who "favored" each other.

I sent the pictures to my friend, Yoshalan. I knew I could trust her opinion; she always told me the truth. She said I looked like Melvin, but then she said, "but you also look like Rosalina too." She explained that I had some features of both Rosalina and Melvin but looked more like Rosalina, but she was sure I was Melvin's child just by looks.

Now I needed clarity and direction on approaching this very touchy subject with Melvin. I reached out to my search angel, Sue. She said she was crossing her fingers that

Melvin was my father. She ran a Been Verified report to look closer into Melvin's background, which suggested that Melvin had children.

She warned me that some siblings may not be receptive or can be scared away and to be careful how I approach the situation. She suggested that I reach out to Melvin's children first, but to be sure not to tell them that I thought Melvin was my father. She also suggested that I ask one of his children to take a DNA test.

I sent Venies a picture of Melvin, and she replied that I have his nose. She suggested that I try writing Melvin a personal letter to "open the door," so to speak, and let him go from there. She also suggested that I tell him that I am not looking for anything, just confirmation that he was my father and that I do not, in any way, shape, or form, want to disrupt his family.

Venies thought I should mention Rosalina's name and let him piece it together when I was conceived. She wondered if I should send a picture of Rosalina and me to Melvin. She said, **"He may or may not respond."** Most importantly, she said, **"Remember, be patient."**

Now I wanted to immediately pick up the phone and call Melvin to say, "I'm your daughter," but I knew I had to go about this in a way not to scare him off and get confirmation before just assuming he was my father. I had to think, regroup, and determine how to not to interrupt his life or family. I had to put the ball in his court and accept whatever happened from this point on.

I was humbled and grateful for all the help and advice I had received from my search angels up to this point. I knew that search angels often had gone through their journeys before helping others, so I knew they spoke from their heart and experience. I knew that one day I would be assisting someone as their search angel.

I thought, who was better to know if this was the man, she had been with so many years ago than my birth mother, Rosalina. I sent her a picture of Melvin and asked her if he was who she remembered, and she responded, no, that is not him.

At first, I was a little disappointed, but I remembered that she told me that she had only seen him once. I accepted her response and continued with my efforts to confirm if Melvin was my father or not.

I looked through Melvin's friend list on Facebook and decided to message someone on his list. I hoped that I would find someone willing to talk to me. I chose Anita and sent her a detailed message on Facebook Messenger regarding my search.

I was sure to give Anita as many details as possible to allow her to decide if she wanted to help me or not. I asked her if Melvin was her father, and she said, **"No, he is my uncle."** Melvin's brother, Ronnie, was Anita's father. I also asked if he had been to the Philippines, but she said she did not know.

I explained to Anita that my DNA matched her relatives, Quintin and his mother, Delores, and that I thought Melvin was my birth father. Anita wasn't familiar with the names Quintin and Delores, and she said she didn't know much about her father's side of the family.

I sent Anita screenshots of the progress I had made from the family tree on Ancestry.com and the pictures of Melvin and my son. She was shocked and thought my son had a strong resemblance to Melvin and her family; however, she was cautious before providing too much information without knowing me, which I understood.

Anita thought I could try and confirm if Melvin is my father through other ways. She gave me a little history of her and her own father's relationship. I appreciated that she shared this information with me, a stranger.

Anita and I also thought we resembled each other. I could not believe how much we looked alike, especially in some of my older pictures when I was younger. She told me that I looked like a "Harris" which meant a lot coming from a part of Melvin's immediate family.

Anita suggested that I move forward and get the answers I needed. This gave me a sense of approval from her, and I knew that we were on the right track. She remained supportive and told me she would try to answer any questions I had.

After speaking to Anita, the shock of realizing that we had just found my birth father was sinking in. All our efforts were finally paying off. My emotions exploded all at once. I was overwhelmed with emotions and began to cry uncontrollably, something I never really did before.

I felt good to release these emotions at that very moment, feelings I had held in for so long. This all seemed surreal; I could not believe that I was so close to knowing the truth, and it all felt good.

I visited Melvin's Facebook page often to see if I could find any other clues about him that would help confirm if he were my father or not. However, nothing on his page indicated if he was previously in the military or had ever been to the Philippines.

I often stared at his picture, wondering if he ever knew about me. I wondered if he was a nice guy and what his life was like. He did not post a lot of information on his Facebook page, and I could not tell if he was married or not. I knew that if he was married, I had to approach everything delicately to ensure I did not create problems within his marriage.

I was excited when Quintin messaged me and asked me my mother's name. Quintin had reached out to Melvin, telling him about me, and Melvin asked about my mother. After I told Quintin my mother's name is Rosalina or Rosie. Quintin responded by saying that Melvin said he does not know your mother and he does not want to be contacted. I was heartbroken.

I thought how could this man not want to know more about a child out there that may be his? I felt hurt and rejected, but I was reminded that this was not only my truth but also his truth, and he had the right to say yes or no.

The lump in my throat swelled as I tried to fight back the tears once again. I wondered how someone could say no without hearing what I had to say. I was not sure what to do next. I had at least hoped that I could confirm if Melvin were my father or not, even if he did not want a relationship with me. But now, I wasn't even going to get that chance.

I did not want to make Melvin any more upset than he already was, so I decided to make one last-ditch effort and write a heartfelt letter to him. This letter would be my only chance to get him open to the possibility that I may be his daughter. I asked Quintin if he would deliver my letter to him, and he said he would.

Four Page Letter

Writing a letter to my potential birth father would be hard and emotional, especially after hearing about his reaction of having a possible child out there. It brought me back to a time in my life over twenty years ago when I wrote the same letter to my birth mother, Rosalina. I was much younger then and struggled with writing the letter, but it all felt the same.

Now, I was reopening the pain I had masked over the years and digging down deep inside to find the right words for a letter to my potential birth father, the only chance I may have to explain myself. It is hard to know exactly what to say in the letter, a story I had so easily told others before. I wondered if I were ready for whatever response I would get, good or bad. I began writing Dear Mr. Melvin.

I tried to think of words that would touch Melvin's heart, which would allow him to want to know if I was his daughter. I knew I had to be sure to say everything I wanted to say this first time because this might be my only chance. Before I knew it, the letter was four pages long; I had spilled my heart out and written what I thought would be my first letter to my birth father.

The letter explained my story, my intentions with writing the letter, my life, and my hopes of finding, meeting, and having a relationship with my birth father and his family. I also explained that if he was my father, it was his choice to move forward or not.

I was both honest and transparent as I explained that I would step back if he chose not to get to know me, but I asked that he allow his family to make their own decision if they wanted to get to know my children and me or not. At the end of the letter, I asked him to take a DNA test to confirm our relationship, I said I would pay for the test.

I had received so much support from family and friends about the letter. Some people offered advice about what I should include, while others said a little prayer for me. My friend, Yoshalan, who had been with me on this entire journey, gave me her honest opinion about my letter and helped me make changes. She even shared information about her personal experience with her father.

My cousin, Di Shawn, whom I had connected with through my journey, asked if I would like him to edit my letter, and I was beyond excited to have him help.

After he read my letter, Di Shawn and I laughed about the part where I told Melvin to take as much time as needed. Di Shawn said, **"For all we know, that could be several years!"** Di Shawn explained that I had indicated earlier in the letter that "life is short" which established a great sense of urgency. Di Shawn wished me the best and told me that he and his wife were here with me no matter the outcome.

One would think the hardest part of writing the letter would be knowing exactly what to say, but I found it just as hard to mail the letter off. After writing it, I held on to the letter a few days, wondering if this was the best way to go about this.

I thought I should just show up on his doorstep with a DNA test and say, I'm your long-lost daughter, let's confirm, or just call him and have an honest conversation with him. I knew that I wanted to know if Melvin was my father, but I didn't know how to take no for an answer.

I had to be okay enough within myself to know that I was enough and worth it no matter the outcome. I know my life had meaning and purpose regardless of what happens after this point. I felt that I too had the right to know who I was and where I came from.

I thought about my journey up to this point, and my focus remained that my children and their children know their roots. I knew that I needed answers for the generations after me. It was as if I could feel the ancestors pushing me to connect the links. Suddenly, I had motivation to do what needed to be done, so, I mailed the letter.

On April 5, 2019, Quintin messaged me and said that he received my letter and left Melvin a voicemail to call him back. I had asked Quintin to read the letter before giving it to Melvin to make sure it sounded okay, and he replied, **"I think it was everything that you needed to say that would make him want to take the test; I am**

praying that he does." I was happy that Quintin approved the letter.

Over the next few days, I waited patiently for a response regarding the letter. I was anxious to find out if Melvin had received and read the letter yet. I did not want to keep bothering Quintin about it, so I waited for him to reach out to me. Eventually, Quintin called and told me that he had "good news and bad news."

God's Perfect Timing

"Timing is everything." – Buck Brannaman

Everything depended on the letter I had written to Melvin, and I needed to convince him to take a DNA test. I could not wait any longer; I had to know what Melvin thought about my letter. If he decided not to take the DNA test, I might never know if he was my birth father.

Quintin called me, and I was so anxious; I sat quietly on the other end of the phone, listening as Quintin explained what happened when he contacted Melvin. Based on Melvin's first reaction to learning about me, I wasn't sure what to expect.

I took a deep breath; Quintin explained that the bad news was that he spoke to Melvin and told him he had a letter I had written that he wanted to give him. He said that Melvin got upset and yelled, "I DON'T WANT THE LETTER!"

At that moment, I could have burst out crying on the phone, but I held it together, and the lump in my throat came quickly. My eyes began swelling up with tears, but I couldn't let Quintin hear me cry.

It was hard to imagine that this was it; I may never know if Melvin was my father or not. We had searched long and hard for my birth father, and to be rejected broke my heart in a million pieces. Hearing Quintin say this was one of the biggest brick walls I hit yet, and I felt hopeless and heartbroken.

Quintin then said the good news is that Melvin's daughter, Nikki, was in the background during the phone call, and she had heard everything that was said. He said Nikki got on the phone with him and said she wanted to talk to me and take the DNA test.

Quintin asked me if he could share my phone number with Nikki, and I was screaming inside, "YES!!" but I calmly replied yes. I could not believe what I was hearing. To know that Nikki, Melvin's daughter, wanted to know if I was her sibling and she was willing to take a DNA test meant everything.

After the call, I reflected on what Quintin had just told me. I did not know if I should be happy or sad. It was hard to be unhappy about Melvin's response, knowing I still had a chance to have answers because Melvin's daughter was willing to test. Nikki didn't know it just yet, but she was my saving grace and the answer to my prayers.

It did not matter how I got confirmation that Melvin was my father, just that I got confirmation. And if he decided he did not want to be a part of my life, it would be something I had to accept.

Soon after I hung up the phone with Quintin, my phone rang from a number I did not recognize; I wondered if it was Nikki. I had little time to prepare, but I answered the phone, and it was Melvin's daughter, Nikki. I said hello, and she replied, "I hear happiness in your voice."

One of my biggest worries throughout this journey was how I would convince my potential birth father or his family members to hear my story, let alone take a DNA test. I know that family members can be very protective of their loved ones, especially when a stranger comes knocking at their door claiming to be their long-lost relative.

Fortunately, it did not take a lot to convince Nikki to test; she explained that she had heard about my story from her family and was curious if this was true. She told me that she had always said she would want to know if she did have a sibling out there because she was her father's only biological child.

Nikki explained that growing up, her father would jokingly say that he would not be surprised if he had another child out there. As I told her my story, she remembered hearing her father mention "Subic" as in Subic Naval Base, where I was born. Again, I thought to myself, the puzzle pieces fit together perfectly.

Nikki explained that she was so open to the idea that I might be her sister, and she wanted to find out for sure. She must have heard the nervousness in my voice because she told me not to worry and that we would figure this out. Nikki agreed to take an Ancestry DNA test, and on April 19, 2019, I wasted no time mailing her a DNA test.

Nikki kept me updated with the progress of her DNA test. I wanted to ask her about the results every day, but I did not want to scare her away. I waited patiently for her text or phone call, although I was on pins and needles the entire time.

Over the next few weeks, I waited for Nikki's DNA test to be processed. I logged onto Ancestry's website several times a day, checking to see if the results were in and if she showed up as a sibling match to me. My friends, family, search angels waited as well, asking me if the results were in. The wait was intense.

On May 6, 2019, I logged onto Ancestry, and to my surprise, Nikki's DNA results were in; however, she was not listed as my sister; she was listed as my first cousin. My heart sank, but I was happy to confirm we were related. However, this was another brick wall, and now that Nikki's DNA results did not show up as her and I being half-siblings, our relationship was unclear. I was confused.

I knew from my Facebook groups that Ancestry.com was a little off on their relationship estimates. And I had once heard that Ancestry.com does not recognize sibling matches. I needed guidance from my search angels.

I reached out to Sue about Nikki's results. She thought it was weird that the amount of DNA I shared with Nikki was not enough for half-siblings but seemed too high for a half first cousin.

LaDona wondered if I could now convince Melvin to test since the results were unclear. She also asked if Melvin had a "secret sibling" that no one knew about and if that sibling could be my father.

Despite the results, LaDona was still confident that Nikki was my sister. She explained how the average worked per Blake, a genealogist, and how the low threshold for half-siblings was 1300, based on 187 matches. LaDona had also been assisting three of my close DNA matches with their search, and since they were also a DNA match to Melvin and Nikki, she felt all our numbers fit perfectly for Melvin to be my father.

Venies explained that Nikki could still be my half-sister but with low centimorgans (amount of DNA). Ancestry.com fails to recognize siblings' relationships and only lists siblings as cousins. She told me not to worry, and she was still sure that Nikki's father was my birth father.

The reassurance from my search angels that Nikki is more than likely my half-sibling helped me realize that there was still a possibility. I wondered how we would narrow it down and hoped we could figure out something fast.

To my surprise, Nikki called to tell me that Melvin had agreed to take a DNA test. She told me that she recently had to return home for a funeral and that she and her cousin, Anita, were able to talk to Melvin about testing. She said they both asked him to test, and his response was, "I'm down!"

I was ecstatic about this news, but I had to keep cool. I could not believe that Melvin had agreed to test. After his response about not contacting him and that he did not want my letter, I thought he wanted nothing to do with all of this.

Nikki and Anita convinced Melvin to take a DNA test, and on May 7th, I sent Melvin a DNA test and waited for the results to come in. If I were Melvin's daughter, surely the Ancestry DNA results would list our relationship as parent and child.

Days seemed long as I waited for Melvin's results to come in. The wait was just as intense as it was when Nikki tested. I was even more anxious for Melvin's results to come back since they would confirm what we all wanted to know. What would the results reveal? Would Melvin be my father, or would I continue searching for my birth father?

I often reflected on my journey up to this point. I have met and spoken with so many people along the way. One name that continued to come up throughout my search was Samantha (Sam). I never really followed up with Samantha, and while I waited for Melvin's test results, I figured now would be a great time.

LaDona encouraged me to reach out to Samantha several times, and she eventually connected us through Facebook. Samantha and I talked on the phone, and I learned about her fascinating story. My search angels had mentioned Samantha's name as a lead, and Samantha had matched some of my DNA matches.

Samantha explained that she felt that our connection was through my birth father and her mother's paternal side. She explained that her mother, Ms. Willie B, had already passed away but that she had always had a desire to discover her family connections. Samantha expressed that she wanted to get the answers her mother had always hoped for.

I was saddened by Samantha's story, that her mother was no longer here, but happy that God allowed

Samantha and me to connect. She was on a path to discover the identity of her maternal grandfather. Our stories tied in somewhere close but getting the answers may be difficult.

I became more eager than ever to get Melvin's DNA results back. I now knew that getting my DNA results and the answers I needed was now more than about me; I realized my journey might help someone else. I knew that I wanted to help Samantha with her journey, and I was up for the challenge.

I continued to log on to Ancestry.com several times a day to check the status, and although a part of me felt like I already knew the answer, we all still needed confirmation. Everyone had their fingers crossed, and we prayed the results would be in soon.

I often thought about what would happen next when the results came in. Would Melvin want me in his life and accept me as his daughter? Would I have a relationship with Nikki but not Melvin?

On June 8, 2019, I received a text from my cousin, Trina, who I had connected with through Ancestry.com. She was asking if I had logged on to the website today. I had not logged on since the night before, but I knew that her text was a good sign.

Trina had helped with my search and was also waiting to see what the DNA results would reveal. We were both curious about our connection to each other, and we hoped the results would help us figure out how our families connected. Trina's text read, **"Log onto Ancestry, the results are in!"**

From reading Trina's text, I started hyperventilating while trying to remain calm, and my fingers shaking as I searched through my phone for the Ancestry.com app.

I swiped through my apps; time seemed to be moving in slow motion. I said a quick prayer and found a quiet area in my house. I took a deep breath. This was the moment that everyone had been waiting for.

As I logged into my account, my eyes quickly moved to the top of my DNA match list. Ms. Deloris, Melvin's Aunt, had recently been at the top of my DNA matches until Nikki tested, but now there was a new match. And there he was, Melvin, at the top of my DNA matches. I stared at the results in shock, wondering if I was reading this right; the results showed that Melvin and I shared 3319 centimorgans of DNA across 129 segments.

All I knew was that the centimorgans number was high; it meant we shared a large amount of DNA and were closely related, but how close. From the Facebook DNA groups, I knew that a number so high usually meant a parent/child relationship and that a child usually shares half of their DNA with each parent.

I didn't want to jump to conclusions before knowing for sure. I looked under the number to see Ancestry's relationship suggestion, and it noted Melvin as a "Parent/Child" relationship to me.

At that moment, everything seemed so surreal. It was as if time stopped for a minute to allow me to focus on that very moment. Everything went silent, and a calm came over me. I couldn't believe what I was reading. I kept re-checking it to ensure that I was not making a mistake.

Still shaking, I sent a text to Nikki, my now half-sister. I told her to check the results, that they were in. I also sent messages to my family, friends, and search angels. I was just as happy for them as I was for me; they had been a part of my journey. I knew that without their help, it would not have happened.

Tears of joy I had held in all these years began to fall. I felt the weight I carried on my shoulders for so long lifted at that instant. I felt the void in my heart healing.

At that moment, I did not care that he might not accept me as his daughter or want to get to know my children and me; it was not even about that. I was celebrating, finally knowing who he was, and nothing could take that moment away from me. I was Melvin's daughter! He was my father! I wanted to scream to the world, "I found my father!!!"

I thought about how my heart could begin to heal from being left without my parents to finding my parents. I thought about my life, my children, and what this meant to our family.

I also thought about all the years I had missed with Melvin and his family, how I could never get those years back, or how I would never meet his family members who had already passed away. I thought about the future and if Melvin and his family would be a part of our lives.

I thought about the people I met along the way to help make this dream come true. All the support I had received from family, friends, and strangers would not go unnoticed. I thought about the support I had received from my search angels and DNA cousins, who encouraged me to keep going no matter how dim the light looked.

I thought about the people who sent me encouraging words or silently prayed that I would find the answers I was looking for. I thought about the strangers that shared their similar stories with me or offered a bit of advice.

I thought about my adopted parents, who gave me a chance at a great life, and how I could never repay them. I thought about how my siblings who passed away couldn't share my joy with me. I thought about my brother, Mike, who I knew related to what I had gone through. I even thought about Melvin and his family and what this meant for them.

I was grateful for that very moment; God led me to my mother, and now my father without a name or any information about him. I was grateful for the search, the journey, and how not only was I finding my birth parents, but I was finding myself. I sat quietly and thanked God for his grace and mercy.

This moment was ***God's perfect timing***! And God knew that as Rosalina left me in the orphanage, on adoption day, when I raised my hand for the pledge of allegiance, when I discovered my birth and adoption records, the moment I found my birth mother, when I submitted my DNA, when I connected with people along this journey or even last year when I was ready to give up, that the perfect time to find my father was now. He had already known the day I would find my family.

I was incredibly grateful for Quintin and his mother, Ms. Delores; I may still be looking for my father without their DNA tests and Quintin's family tree on Ancestry.com. They tried their best to help get me the answers I needed.

I was thankful for my DNA cousins for all that they did to help me to the very end, even without knowing their exact relationship to me. I was beyond grateful for my new sister and cousin, who helped convince Melvin to test, which gave me the answers I so desperately needed.

My husband and children were excited about the news. They knew I had spent a long time chasing a dream that I was not always sure would come true, but they remained supportive and were excited to know they had newfound family.

I was so happy to know that I finally had the answers, but I was quickly reminded that initially, Melvin was not happy about this whole idea of having a child out there. I wondered how I would tell my children that I was not sure that Melvin wanted to be a part of our lives.

I wondered if Melvin would have a change of heart now that the results showed that he was my father. I knew I had to approach this and not push him further away. I knew my journey was not over just yet, and once again, I was up for the challenge.

Forty-three years had passed of Melvin not knowing about me, and how would I convince him that I needed and wanted him in my life? How do you tell someone you were not taking no for an answer when the choice was up to them? What could I do or say to change his mind? It would not be easy to convince him to have a relationship with me if he were already skeptical about the whole situation.

Facebook was like an outlet for me to express my feelings, and I had always been so open about my journey. I felt like no one judged me there, and if they did, it was behind a computer or phone screen. I was vulnerable on Facebook but also transparent. I enjoyed the feedback, positive and negative, with sharing my story and hearing other people's advice and their own experiences, which helped a lot.

My latest post on Facebook read, "Being adopted is like having blank pages in the first chapter of your book." This was truly the experience I had for so many years, I was adopted at 18 months old, and I knew nothing about the beginning of my life.

After posting my DNA results, someone sent me a message on Messenger that knew Melvin that read, **"I know your dad, and if he had known you, you wouldn't be adopted, I hope you can forgive him."**

To hear that I would have been wanted and not abandoned started to help me heal. It felt good to hear someone say that, especially someone that knows Melvin personally. And despite what he was feeling, knowing that things might have been different if he had known about me helped me realize that I may have been wanted.

Since learning about the DNA results, Nikki and I had begun communicating more. She immediately accepted my family into her heart.

Nikki was an instant Aunt to my five children, and I had gained a niece and nephew. She told me that Melvin had adopted a son who lived near me in California. I was happy to hear he chose to adopt.

Now that the results were in, I had hoped that Melvin would reconsider and immediately pick up the phone to call me. I waited and waited, but he never called. I wondered if he would ever reach out to me; I had not prepared myself for rejection after the DNA results, but I knew it was a possibility.

I tried to put myself in Melvin's shoes to understand that finding out that you have a daughter after all these years would have hurt anyone, and I knew that he needed time to process everything. I hope he didn't blame himself; he had no control over what had happened.

I could only imagine the guilt he must have felt, but if I could have talked to him, I wanted him to know that I didn't blame him, and it wasn't his fault. I wanted him to know that being adopted was one of the best things that happened to me.

Although I wanted to call Melvin or show up on his doorstep, I decided I would give him time to process everything by not contacting him first. I wanted our first conversation to be on his terms, no matter how long it took. I held back from reaching out to him to allow him this time to determine if he wanted to get to know me or not. I left the ball in his court and allowed him to make the next move.

A few months went by without hearing from Melvin; it hurt to realize that he was not as excited or anxious to talk to me as I was. The feelings I had were of rejection and hurt.

No one else from his family reached out to me. I felt lost and confused about what to do next. I hurts to think that my birth father may not want me in his life.

I reached out to my sister, Nikki, about Melvin contacting me, and she said that Melvin felt guilty about all the years that have gone by and not knowing about me.

Nikki said she told Melvin he would not have known, and it was not his fault, but she assured me that he would eventually come around. I was sad to know he was hurting behind all of this, but I knew once he took the opportunity to get to know me, he would feel better.

I reached out to my newfound cousin, Anita, Melvin's niece. She had also welcomed me into the family with open arms. I felt that before we knew the DNA results and confirmed we were cousins, she had already accepted me.

In August 2019, I received a call from an unknown number. I usually did not answer calls from unknown numbers, but I wondered if this was the call I had been waiting for from Melvin. I thought if it is him, what do I say, what do I do? Maybe I wasn't ready to talk to him like I thought I was.

Nikki had told me that she had given my number to Sandra (Sandy), Melvin's sister, but I completely forgot. Aunt Sandy lives in Albuquerque, New Mexico, and called to meet me over the phone. I answered the phone, a lady's voice said, "Hello Jennifer, this is your Aunt Sandy, Melvin's sister."

I was beyond excited to hear from one of Melvin's family members. Although this wasn't Melvin calling me, I was just as happy that his sister reached out to me. Aunt Sandy told me she had heard about me and asked Nikki for my phone number. She welcomed me into the family, and we talked for a long time.

During our conversation, Aunt Sandy told me about the family, the good and bad times. She talked about some relatives who had passed on, including her father, Johnnie, and four of her siblings, Greta, Carolyn, Ronnie, and Kenneth. She said I would have loved my Aunt Greta and Carolyn, and she knows they would have loved me too.

Aunt Sandy talked about other relatives who were still living, including her son, a photographer, and Aunt Lois (Aunt Deloris). She mentioned that although she is not that close with everyone, she stays in contact with her mother, and she mostly saw and talked to the rest of the family when she would go home to Cincinnati for visits.

Aunt Sandy explained how blessed I was to have Melvin as my father. She said that Melvin is who I would want to be my father out of all her brothers because Melvin was so nurturing and loving. She said she was unsure where Melvin had learned to be this way, but God must have made him this way.

Aunt Sandy told me stories about how Melvin moved from California to Ohio with Nikki and how Nikki got her name. She said, "I know that if Melvin would have known about you, he would have got you. You would have never been left there." It meant a lot to hear her tell me this.

The thought of what Aunt Sandy said made me wonder what my life would have been like if I was never given up for adoption and was given to Melvin. It was a little sad to think I would have missed out on all the people in my life now.

Although, Aunt Sandy was not Melvin, she was his sister, and it felt good to feel accepted into her heart. We exchanged pictures through texts, and we promised to meet each other soon.

During another phone call with Aunt Sandy in August, she told me that Anita and her mother, Mabel, were going to a family reunion in South Carolina. She said that Melvin was supposed to take his mother to the reunion, but he had hurt himself and was not attending the reunion.

When Aunt Sandy explained that this was the McQueen family reunion in Cheraw, South Carolina, I recognized the name. This was the same reunion Ms. Gladys had previously invited me to, and if I would have gone, I would have met my new grandmother and cousin, Anita.

I would later discover that Granny Mabel and Ms. Gladys were cousins who grew up together. God had put me in touch with Ms. Gladys when searching for Melvin, and she tried to help me figure out who my father was, but it never crossed her mind that my father was her cousin Mabel's son. I continued to stay keep in touch with Ms. Gladys.

Over the next few weeks, I never heard from Melvin, and I had accepted that Melvin and I were not going to connect. I had wondered why his mother had not reached out to me either.

In October 2019, my family and I traveled to Killeen, Texas, to visit my daughter, I'Layia, after the birth of her first son, Devon, my third grandson.

Since we were driving to Texas, I decided that this would be the perfect opportunity for my children and me to meet my new sister and her family, especially since we were passing through Phoenix, Arizona, where she lived. I was excited that this would give us a little time to get to know one another.

As I pulled up to my sister's home, I was nervous and anxious about what her first impression of me would be. I know that meeting a new sibling under these circumstances had to be a lot. I prayed that our meeting went well.

Seeing Nikki for the first time, I was flooded with emotions. She seemed to already love and accept me, and I did too. We hugged, and she gave me a big kiss.

I was excited to meet my new niece, Nae'Ja, my nephew, Cameron, and my step-niece, Tamiea. Nikki also introduced me to one of her best friends, Kenny, who was like a brother.

After introducing ourselves, Nikki handed me her phone. I looked at the cell phone bewildered, wondering who was on the phone. The person on the other end said hello. I immediately knew it was my father, Melvin. Nikki had called him so that we could finally talk.

Although our first conversation was brief, I was happy to finally know that Melvin was at least open to talking to me. He tried to apologize for not being in my life, but I told him he did not have to apologize and that it was not his fault.

Melvin told me to get his phone number from Nikki and call him anytime. After I got off the phone with Melvin, I was excited to know that I had just talked to my father for the first time, and this was the start of something good.

We were fortunate enough to stop by Nikki's house again in Phoenix on our way home from Texas for a second visit. I was just as excited to see her as I was the first time we stopped.

While there, Nikki cooked us dinner and we also met Nikki's children's father, Junay. Our kids played together, and we spent more time together getting to know one another.

Just like my previous visit, Nikki handed me her phone. I wondered if Melvin was calling me again. However, this time it was not Melvin; it was Nikki's mother, Ms. Debra.

I said hello and Ms. Debra said was, "I gained another daughter." We talked briefly, and I told her I was looking forward to meeting her one day. Nikki's mother lived in the Bay Area, only a couple of hours from where I lived in California.

Although my visits with my new sister were brief, we had a great time starting our sisterly bond. We promised to visit each other. I was thankful that God had allowed me this time with my sister.

One day, my phone rang, and I saw Melvin's number show up on my phone's screen. I had already added his number to my contacts, hoping one day he would call. I did not hesitate to answer the phone; I would not miss this call, like I missed Rosalina's call many years ago.

Melvin was so easy to talk with. It was as if I was talking to a long-lost friend. He seemed down to earth and interested in getting to know me. We talk about our families and his military days. He told me that his mother, Mabel, was 89 years old.

Melvin also talked about meeting my children and grandchildren. He asked me to give them his phone number to call him. I was so excited to know that he wanted to meet my children. This meant everything to me.

Our conversation went well, and Melvin seemed genuinely happy to know he had another daughter. I worried about what to call him, Melvin, or Dad? Just like any new relationship, it was going to take some time getting used to, but I knew this meant that he accepted me and wanted to be in my life.

After speaking to Melvin, I decided I did not want to waste more time meeting him and his mother. I called Nikki and suggested that we plan a trip to Cincinnati together soon so that I could meet everyone in person, and she agreed.

Welcome to Cincinnati

"Never put off till tomorrow what may be done day after tomorrow just as well." - Mark Twain

artin Luther King Jr.'s (MLK) birthday weekend, January 18, 2020, I flew to Cincinnati, Ohio, to meet my father for the first time. I wanted to celebrate change; it had always been constant in my life. And because Dr. King represented change with his message of freedom, equality, justice, and love, I felt this would be the perfect time for this special time in my life.

In the weeks leading up to my visit to Cincinnati, I was a nervous wreck. I held it together, believing that this was what Melvin wanted. However, I started having second thoughts, thinking maybe I was rushing things.

As the days got closer, my emotions were everywhere. It was hard even to focus while at work, knowing that my life would once again change forever, and I would finally open and close a new chapter in my life within a few short days.

It's funny how you can go through everything to search and find someone, but you start to have second thoughts when it comes down to the first meeting. I was overjoyed that I had found my birth father, but the fact remained that meeting him in a few days was starting to weigh heavily on me. I do not know if I were worried about what he would think about me or what to say, but I began to feel overwhelmed with everything that was happening.

I had to keep telling myself that Melvin and his family were happy that I found them and that they had accepted me. I could not allow negative thoughts to consume me. I reminded myself of all the work we had put in to make this day happen, and it was finally happening.

I reached out to my family and friends and talked to them about the feelings that I was having leading up to meeting Melvin. Three of my coworkers, Teresa, Niema, and Lisa, were godsends, and they continuously supported me up until the day of my flight. We even set up "lunch counseling sessions" a few days before to allow me to ask "what if" questions about what to expect. I am sure they thought I was crazy, but they were all open and willing to share their own experiences with their fathers. In the end, they encouraged me just to be myself.

As I prepared for the trip, I called my new great aunt Deloris (Aunt Lois), Quintin's mother. I wanted to be sure that she and Quintin knew I was coming to Cincinnati so that I could have a chance to meet them.

Aunt Lois and Quintin played a big part in finding Melvin, and I wanted to thank them both in person. Aunt Lois was excited that I was coming and told me not to worry, that she would be sure to make plans to meet me while I was there.

My search angel, LaDona, who had been with me until the end, was excited that I was going to Cincinnati to meet Melvin. She was so funny, she said, "And ask her (Granny Mabel) who her father was, the Boyd or someone else?" LaDona was still committed to having the correct information on the family tree, even after the results were in.

Before my flight to Cincinnati, I was on social media, and I noticed a post from my little brother, Sammy, Rosalina's son. He stated in the post that he had just moved from San Diego to Cincinnati. I had not seen my younger brother since my sister's funeral back in 2016, and what were the odds that Sammy had just moved to Cincinnati, and I was flying there in less than two days to meet my birth father. I knew I had to make time to see Sammy, God's perfect timing.

On the day of my flight, I worked half a day to ensure that I made the redeye flight out of San Francisco on time. I could not stop thinking that early the next morning my life will change forever, and I will have finally met my birth father.

My flight arrived at Cincinnati/Northern Kentucky International Airport (CVG) at 5:00 am, so I had plenty of time to think about what to say to Melvin. I could not sleep much during the flight because I was too anxious about what to expect. I kept playing out scenarios in my head about seeing Melvin for the first time; I did not even notice the turbulence on the plane as my mind stayed focused on what was going to happen in the next few hours.

I wondered if I should hug Melvin or shake his hand. What if he does not like hugging? What do I say, or

195

JenniferRose Davis

should I wait for him to say something first? I had many questions, but I did not have much longer to think about it because my flight had landed.

My sister's flight had arrived early, and she called and said that they (she and Melvin) were outside the airport waiting to pick me up. I would see my father for the first time in the next few minutes.

I thought maybe I could get a glimpse of him before we met. It was still dark outside, so I could not see anything through the windows in the baggage area. I could barely focus on getting my luggage from the baggage area.

The walk from the baggage area to Melvin's car seemed long, although it was just outside the door. As I walked, I briefly thought about my first meeting with Rosalina and how things differed. I thought about my children, who I wish were here to be a part of this amazing experience. Finally, I remembered to thank God for allowing me this opportunity to finally meet my father.

This was it! I was about to meet Melvin, and there was no turning back. As I took each step toward his car, it represented all the no's and brick walls I had faced while searching for him. Each step I took was if the ancestors surrounded me, encouraging me, guiding me towards the car, and cheering me on as I was about to link the chains of my family to his family.

As I got closer to Melvin's car, I knew that at that very moment, I would no longer wonder who I was and where I came from. It is as if somehow the hands of time would briefly stop and shift gears to begin my new life of knowing my father and his family.

196

Melvin got out of the car and came around the car to hug me. It was my first hug with my father and meant the world to me. I no longer questioned who or why. I wanted to cry, but I held it in because I could never let anyone see me cry. A calmness came over me again, and I knew God was telling me everything would be all right and that I did not have to wonder anymore.

The drive through Cincinnati on the way to Melvin's home was nice. It was early in the morning and still dark outside. The lights from the city's skyline lit up downtown Cincinnati making it one of the most beautiful skylines I had ever seen. The view was perfect and fitting for the moment; it was a view I would never forget. It was as if the city was saying, welcome home Jennifer.

We passed by the Cincinnati Bengals stadium, and I got a glimpse of the Ohio River as the moonlight beamed off the water. A big Ferris wheel demanded its share of the city's spectacular view, and buildings stood tall and strong in the heart of the Queen City, my father's city.

We arrived at Melvin's house, and I was excited to see where he lived. His 89-year-old mother, my grandmother (Granny Mabel), also lived with him.

Up to this point, everything I learned about Melvin was either through my sister, other family members, or from his Facebook profile. But standing here in front of his house, in the city he was born and raised in, was overwhelming. I had always wondered where my father was from and where he lived and now, I knew.

197

Melvin helped me with my luggage and showed me the room I would be staying in during my visit. The room was upstairs. I settled in the room, but I could not sleep, so I sat on the sleeper for a moment to take it all in.

Melvin came to the room a few minutes later and sat down next to me on the couch. He smiled and said, "Tell me everything, I want to know everything."

I was caught off guard since it was so early in the morning; I assumed he might go back to bed, but this made my heart so happy. It was nice to know that he wanted to learn more about me, my life, and my family. I did not hesitate to tell him my story, beginning with being born in the Philippines.

As I began telling my story, I knew this time would be different. I had told this story many times before, but I could feel the weight being lifted off my shoulders as I talked to him about what my life had been like being adopted and not knowing my birth parents. I explained how I had a great life and didn't regret anything up to this point in my life. Once again, the ancestors gathered around us listening, as I told him everything about my life.

Melvin listened intensely, even comparing the dates I mentioned when I was born and living in California. He said, "Yes, that sounds right." We both laughed. He explained that he had visited the Philippines four times while in the Navy, and the time I was probably conceived was during his second visit to the Philippines. Knowing that he had probably came back to the Philippines after my birth was hard to hear. If he had only known about me.

Melvin was even easier to talk to in person; he was open with telling me everything about his life, and he did not seem to leave anything out. He spoke about growing up in Ohio and his family. Melvin mentioned having a girlfriend during one of the times he visited the Philippines, and at first, when he learned about me, he wondered if his girlfriend was my mother. He explained that his time in the Philippines was his "wild" days, but I understood, and there was no need to explain.

Melvin explained that he was never stationed in the Philippines and was only sent there for R&R (rest and relaxation). He said that he was stationed in Alameda, California, and we both discovered he lived only a few hours from where I grew up in California. It hurt to know that we were only miles away from each other when we both lived in California, but we had no way of knowing about each other.

As I talked about my adoption, Melvin seemed sad and apologized again. I tried to explain that it was not his fault; he would not have known. I told him I know things happen for a reason, and everything was supposed to happen this way. He said, "I just want you to know, if I had known, you would have been with me!"

Melvin was also very sincere about apologizing for reacting like he did when he first learned about me. He said he was hearing different stories from different family members while trying to understand that he might have a child he did not know about.

Melvin said he didn't understand why some of his family members insisted that I was his daughter without even confirming that I was his daughter. He said he wished I had come to him first.

While we continued talking, Granny Mabel had entered the room. She said she tried to stay up until I arrived but fell asleep. Granny joined in on our conversation. She sat down close to me and expressed that she was happy to see me. She listened while Melvin and I continued to talk.

Granny Mabel was so cute and seemed eager to hear everything I had to say about my life. She explained that she did not hear well and asked me to speak up loudly as I told the rest of my story. Sharing this special moment with my father and grandmother, was more than I could have ever asked for.

Granny Mabel's mind was sharp, and she was open with me about her life. She told me stories about each of her seven children, including those who had already passed away and their father, Johnnie.

I was sad to know that I had missed meeting my aunts and uncles, Greta, and Carolyn, who had died years before, and my uncles Ronnie and Kenneth, who had just recently passed a few months before finding Melvin.

Granny Mabel talked about growing up in Tallahassee, Florida. She explained she was the oldest of her siblings and helped raise her siblings after her mother passed away when she was young. She also talked about being raised by her grandmother, Rachel McQueen, and about moving to Cincinnati with her husband.

I learned a lot about Granny Mabel as a mother and grandmother, and it hurt to know I had missed so many years with her. She was eighty-nine, and only God knows how many more years I have left to spend with her. Since tomorrow is never promised, I decided I would make these years count and to be present in her life as much as possible.

Granny Mabel showed me so much love during my first visit. She taught me how to make her cornbread recipe and gave me sentimental things that were once her daughter Carolyn's. She even gave me some pictures to take with me. Granny Mabel pulled out a box of old photos, and she told me stories about each picture which helped me get to know more about the family.

It was so sweet to see Granny Mabel go down memory lane. It was easy to follow along as she talked about her family because I had created her family tree on Ancestry.com long before finding them. I recognized the names of family members she spoke about and her stories. I heard several times from everyone while I was there, you know more about the family than I do.

It was amazing that Granny Mabel came into my life with God's perfect timing when she did. I recently lost my grandmother, Queen, who had died in November 2019, at the age of ninety-six, and I met Granny Mabel in January 2020. So, having Granny Mabel was just the medicine I needed. She fit into my life perfectly, and I was so happy to have her in my life. I felt honored to know her.

While in Cincinnati, my extended family came over to my house for dinner to meet me. I was excited to finally meet my cousin, Quintin, his wife, Shelia, his mother, my Aunt Deloris. That evening, Cousin Shelia gave me my first tour of the city of Cincinnati.

I always wanted to thank Quintin in person for all that he had done with trying to help me with my search and connecting me with Melvin. Aunt Lois invited us over for dinner the next day, and I met more family and took family photos.

During my visit, I also met Melvin's best friend. Gene and Granny Mabel's best friend, Ms. Diane. Ms. Diane had come over to have dinner with us. While she was there, Granny said, "Jennifer, you want to go to the casino?" It was funny because I looked at Melvin, Nikki, and Anita to try and find the best answer to respond to Granny's question, and they all looked at me and said, you might as well get broken in! So, I said yes, and I was off to the casino with two sweet little old ladies.

I enjoyed spending time with my sister during my visit. She introduced me to a few of her friends. Nikki kept me laughing, and it's safe to say we get our sense of humor from Melvin. I was also able to spend more time getting to know my new niece and nephew.

My new cousin, Anita, Melvin's niece, who I had reached out to initially during my search, had also come from Memphis to meet me. Granny Mabel was excited to have three of her granddaughters visiting her.

Anita stayed with us during my visit. I was happy she was there. She took me to her son's birthday party, and I met some of her family and friends.

Over the next three days, we had all bonded so much in a short amount of time, it was as if we tried to fit forty-three years into three short days, but I loved every minute of it. We talked and laughed so much that I felt like I had known them all my life, and they were sure not to leave out any details. They treated me like I had always been there.

I even made time to visit my brother, Sammy, Rosalina's son, who had recently relocated to Cincinnati. I had not seen him in years, and it was great to connect with him again while there. I felt like God put Sammy in my path while visiting Melvin in Cincinnati to remind me that not only did I have my father's family, but also my mother's family.

Time goes by fast when you are having fun, and three days came and went quickly. I kept dreading that my visit would end soon. I was enjoying the time with my new family and learning all about them. On the last day of my visit, I knew I had to prepare to say goodbye.

I wondered how you say goodbye after just saying hello for the first time in forty-three years. I had barely met my new family, and I was sad and wanted to hold on to them forever. I was a little afraid of what saying goodbye really meant.

I had not prepared myself for this moment. I did not know when I would be able to see them again. I promised myself that I would visit as much as possible, and I would not waste any time in planning for my husband and children to meet everyone soon. Unlike Rosalina, she has never met my husband or children and I had given up on the idea that she ever would.

We shared our last few hours doing what I love most, eating and spending time with family. Granny Mabel took us all out to lunch on my last day before my flight left.

I enjoyed my last few hours with my family, and as we said our goodbyes at the airport, I wanted to freeze this moment in time, so I would never forget this moment. I wish we lived closer, so I visit with them every day, but I knew that we all had our own lives to live.

As Melvin and I hugged one last time before my flight at the airport, he said to me, it's okay to call me dad. I was so happy to hear him say those words, and I looked at my sister and saw the approval on her face.

At this moment, I knew God had joined us forever, and I finally had my birth father. I no longer had to wonder if he wanted to be in my life or what to call him; he was now just dad.

God had given me the gift of having two dads. I thought about my father in Houston, and how he wondered if the man I found would be a bad person. It may seem odd to call two people dad, but both hold a special place in my heart. I knew God intended for me to have two dads, and neither would take the place of the other.

After returning home from my visit to Cincinnati, I continued researching my family tree. The puzzle pieces finally fit together perfectly, and, in the end, I had a beautiful picture of my family tree, a complete family tree that included my adoptive and birth family.

I felt like I was beginning to heal and fill the void in my heart. No more questions about who I was or where I came from. I no longer had to wonder if I was loved or remembered.

JenniferRose Davis

Family by Blood

"A mother's hug last long after she lets go." –
Unknown

I was still curious about my ancestors and my family history, so I continued my research even after finding Melvin. There were still several DNA matches that I had not found the connections with, and now that I knew my family line, I hoped that I could find our link.

Samantha, who was a DNA match to Melvin, continued her journey looking for her maternal grandfather. Although, she was not coming up as a match to me on Ancestry.com due to the algorithm, we were a match on FTDNA.com

While visiting my dad in Cincinnati, Samantha drove from Indianapolis, Indiana, where she lived, to meet me in person. We had talked several times on the phone, and we looked forward to meeting one day. This was a perfect time for us to connect, and the first time I had met one of my DNA matches in person, and it was an amazing experience.

Samantha and I had lunch at a local coffee shop called the Taste of Belgium in downtown Cincinnati. It was nice to talk and share our stories. We laughed, cried, and got to know each other during our short visit. I was so happy she took time out of her day to meet me.

Samantha's journey was like mine and what was amazing was that her story included my family line. She was trying to find the identity of her paternal grandfather, who was possibly a great-grand uncle of mine through Melvin. She was a DNA match to my dad, Quintin, and great aunt Lois, on Ancestry.com, which made us believe she was related from the McCary side.

With the help of our search angel, LaDona, who had reached out to Samantha during my search for my dad, we had narrowed down the search to Abe McCary's brothers. We just needed that one clue that would connect us forever.

Samantha's mother, Ms. Willie B, was born and adopted from Evergreen, Alabama. Ms. Willie was biracial, born to a Caucasian mother and a Black father in 1949. However, she passed away before learning the identity of her birth parents, and Samantha had vowed to find the answers to this lifelong mystery in memory of her mother. However, her mother's birth circumstances left Samantha with more questions than answers.

Samantha learned that after her mother was born, her mother's maternal family intended to bury her mother alive as an infant due to being half black. However, before this could happen, two men came to get the baby (Ms. Willie), and they gave her to a woman across town in Evergreen who set up the adoption of the baby.

Supposedly, the baby's father was lynched; however, Samantha could not find confirmation that anyone was hung in Evergreen in 1949, even though not all lynchings were recorded, and finding someone who remembered would be challenging. Samantha felt there was a possibility that her mother's father was never lynched and left town.

I decided to talk to my new Aunt Sandy about Samantha's story. While talking to Aunt Sandy, she felt that Ms. Willie's story tied into the McCary's brothers, Aunt Sandy's great uncles. She stated that she had heard that her grandfather, Abe McCary, and his brothers left Evergreen abruptly in the middle of the night due to unknown issues with a "white woman" around that time.

Was it possible that Ms. Willie's father was not lynched but one of the brothers that left Evergreen to keep from being lynched? The stories seemed eerily similar. We decided to call Aunt Lois to see what she knew about this story.

With Samantha's excellent researching skills and talking with DNA matches we had in common, Samantha seemed closer to learning the identity of her grandfather. She discovered her mother's maternal side through DNA and was able to connect with two aunts she later met in person.

Samantha, also connected to Mr. Willie from Pensacola, Florida, who was the son of one of the McCary brothers, James, through a DNA match. He is eighty-five years old and was willing to help Samantha by talking to us on the phone about her mother's story, with the help of his daughter Marie.

Samantha, Aunt Sandy, and Aunt Lois talked to Mr. Willie on a three-way phone call, but unfortunately, Mr. Willie told them that he had only heard that his uncles had to leave in the middle of the night, but he was never told why. Although Mr. Willie could not tell them a lot of information, he helped tremendously by agreeing to take an Ancestry.com DNA test to confirm how he was related to Samantha.

Mr. Willie's DNA test came back as a match to both Samantha and me; however, we could not discover anything further about Samantha's maternal grandfather from his DNA results. It only confirmed what we already knew; we were related. We were grateful for Mr. Willie's willingness to take a DNA test to try and help her with the answers she so desperately needed.

Samantha continues her journey as she gets closer to finding the identity of her maternal grandfather. Each new DNA match holds some potential information that may help her discover his identity. Her story has led us to meet more relatives from the McCary family line. I do not doubt that Samantha will find out his identity soon. We will both continue to research leads that will one day hopefully point us in the right direction.

In October 2021, Samantha and her family met Cousin Willie and his family during a visit to Pensacola, Florida. Samantha also visited newfound family in Evergreen, Alabama.

We also hoped that discovering my dad would also help another DNA match, Stephania, with the identity of her biological father. We were confident we would have answers, but that was not the case.

By Stephania being a close match to my family, we believe Stephania's father was one of Melvin's uncles, but narrowing it down would take some more work. We continue to revisit leads, and hopefully, we will uncover the truth soon.

Tita Baby

"In the end, it's not the years in your life that count. It's the life in your years." Abraham Lincoln

One day, I was looking over each section of my birth certificate trying to learn more about my birth. It was interesting to see my birth weight and the time I was born. These little details meant so much since I didn't know anything about myself as a baby.

The certificate listed "one" under the section that showed the number of children living and previous deliveries, but I had never noticed it before. There it was, in black and white, I was the second living child born to Rosalina. If I had only read the birth certificate in detail, I would have known I had an older sibling out there, Steven.

I remember Rosalina told me she lived with her aunt and uncle when she moved to Olongapo City. I wondered if the address on my birth certificate was the same as their address. I decided I would research this more to see if I could locate them and just maybe they remembered me as a baby.

Diana, who lives in Olongapo City, was introduced to me by Terrance in the DNA Experts Facebook group. Diana helped Terrance search for his sister. They both helped me search for my dad. Diana was always available to help with anything I needed related to the Philippines.

I sent Diana a private message and showed her a picture of the address in Olongapo City on my birth certificate. She didn't recognize the area and asked me if I wanted her to find Rosalina's aunt and uncle. I said yes with excitement, knowing that we were off on another journey.

Diana was confident that she could find Rosalina's aunt and uncle. She added me to three Philippines Facebook groups where she posted a question asking if anyone knew Norma in that area; she included the address. Within minutes, someone commented that Norma was living at that address, and then another person related to Norma sent Diana a private message.

I was beyond excited to know that Diana may have just found Rosalina's family, the ones we lived with when I was born. Sadly, the person stated that Norma and Rodrigo had passed away and that Norma and Rodrigo were siblings, not spouses.

Shortly after, Diana created a group chat with four of Norma's children, Maricel (48), Ronald (51), Marivic (45), and Maribel (42), and she invited me to join. I was excited to meet Norma's children, and they were all open to talking with me. They explained that their parents had six children, two other siblings who were not on Facebook.

The siblings also explained that Norma and Rolando were their parents and Rodrigo was Norma's brother. They also confirmed that their family lived in Macaraeg, the address on my birth certificate. They went on to say that their mother, Norma, passed away in 2019 at age 75, and their father passed away in 2014 at age 77. They shared pictures with me.

One of the older siblings remembered Rosalina and me when we lived there. She explained that they called Rosalina Tita Baby (Aunt Baby). I was so surprised when she mentioned my brother Steve, who they remembered as a little boy at that time. Maribel asked, whose name was Steve. Ronaldo explained that he remembers riding minibikes with Steve as a child.

It was amazing to find more relatives in the Philippines and even relatives who remember me as a baby. I was happy about this new connection to my family to help complete my journey. And I was thankful for Diana and all the help she had given me throughout my search for my dad and Norma's family.

JenniferRose Davis

A Happy Ending to a New Beginning

"Life is short. Time is fast. No replay. No rewind. So enjoy every moment as it comes." – *Unknown*

For adoptees or anyone searching for their birth family who are blessed to find them, God chose you to carry out this journey in life. For whatever reason, we were the chosen ones, and I was given this *journey to my origin.*

We love and cherish our adoptive families, and by no means does finding our birth family takes away the unconditional love we have for our adoptive families. Their desire to provide us with a loving home and their willingness to accept a child who was not their own could never be replaced. However, we search for our birth families for many different reasons; some want to know their lineage or heritage, others for health reasons. We seek *the treasure at the end*, wanting to fill that void or that emptiness in our hearts.

Only you know if you are ready to make that choice to seek out your birth family, and the choice is only yours to make. And ***defining the unknown*** is your truth.

Every person's adoption experience and reaction are valid and deserve to be their truth. Whether the adoption was at birth or a young age, or someone discovered they were adopted or not related later in life, no two experiences are the same.

It may be challenging for those who find their family to see someone who looks like them or shares similar physical characteristics and personality quirks. An adoptee may start to feel that they are now wanted, or adoptive parents may think that their children are seeking the love of their birth families over them. It also may be hard for the birth parents to get past the guilt of knowing they gave their child up for adoption.

Whatever the reason, your search for your family eventually becomes your journey, and you begin finding yourself, including discovering how strong you are and how you have endured so much. You discover a deeper self-understanding, your purpose, along with a confrontation with reality.

Being prepared for the highs and lows of searching for your family and the emotional roller coaster you will ride, will help when facing brick walls or going down wrong leads throughout your search. Just know that brick walls can be knocked down.

Some birth parents and adopted children may not wish to be found or are unwilling to invest in a relationship with you, while the others have waited for the day you came looking for them. The journey may have you questioning why you are doing this or if it's even worth it but remember, God gave you this journey for a reason.

Circumstances and government policies may also make it challenging to find answers. Uncovering secrets or disturbing memories may jeopardize your search, or it could add closure to already open wounds, but they will begin to heal with closure.

Closure may come in many ways, and closure is different for everyone. Closure for an adoptee could include a meeting with the birth parent, a conversation by phone, or a simple letter, photograph, or card.

Closure could be just knowing who they are, knowing your medical history, and not having that desire to meet birth parents or families. Closure could be having answers to questions you have had all your life, or closure could be the ending to a new beginning. Whatever closure looks like for you; it will help you heal your heart.

Closure for me was about forgiveness. I chose to forgive to release the feelings that kept me consumed throughout my life regarding why my birth parents abandoned me. I knew that I may never know the real answer to why I was given up for adoption, but I had to ask.

Although I had known Rosalina for over twenty years, I had never built up the courage to ask her questions about my birth and adoption. I was always afraid to bring up the topic; I knew it made her uncomfortable, knowing she may not want to revisit that time in her life. However, once I did ask her, I could finally release what had been consuming me all my life.

I reached out to Rosalina via Facebook Messenger, asking her questions about her mother, Lourdes. She explained that she did not know her mother because she left her when she was about three years old. She seemed willing to share what she remembered.

Rosalina explained that her mother had lived in the same town as her, but she never came to see her after she left. I felt sad that Rosalina did not grow up with her mother, and I could relate to her feelings.

Rosalina said she had never been told why her mother left her family, but she thought it was because she had started a new family. She said she was later told that her mother had died, and for years, this is what she believed that her mother was dead.

Reluctantly, I asked Rosalina questions about my adoption. Her response was, **"I'm sorry, I just couldn't take care of you."** Unfortunately, Rosalina could not tell me much, maybe she forgot, or it was too painful to revisit.

We continued to talk and I had hoped to get more information from her about me as a baby, but she said she couldn't remember. I felt like revisiting was getting harder for her to answer my questions or maybe I was digging too deep.

I had always assumed that I was given up for adoption because I was half Black. I asked Rosalina why she had only given me up and if it was because I was Black and her other children were not, and she said, **"No, it's not because you're Black, everyone is the same, Black or**

220

White." I figured it would be hard to admit something like that even if it were true, so I took her answer for what it was worth, her truth.

I apologized to Rosalina for asking so many tough questions, and I told her it still hurt to know she gave me up for adoption. I felt bad for taking Rosalina back to a point in her life she probably wanted to forget. She responded by saying, **"I know I'm so sorry; it hurts me to know that I bring a kid to the world but couldn't take care of it."** She went on to say, **"Believe me, if I could have you to stay and care for you if I had the money, I would."** She said, **"I thank God after all this time we found each other. I love you."**

As much as I wanted to believe that she wanted to keep me, a part of me thought it was better the way things had turned out. There was a reason it happened this way, and instead of questioning it, I trust and know that God covered me in His blood and watched over me. God knew one day I would search and find what I was looking for. I honestly believe *seek, and ye shall find, and God answers the deepest longing in my heart.*

Talking with Rosalina gave me closure. Rosalina was telling what she had told herself for many years. She seemed genuinely sorry for giving me up for adoption. My mother mentioned I should be thankful that Rosalina gave birth to me and did not abort me; and that she also tried to take care of me as long as she did.

Although I wanted to hear Rosalina say yes, I made a mistake, I wanted you, or I wish I would have never left you there, I realized she did what she thought was best at the time. I no longer blame her, and she loved me so much that she made the ultimate sacrifice by giving me up for adoption to have a better life. I could not be mad about that, and now I have answers to help me move forward with this new chapter in my life.

My dad was unaware that I existed, so there were no questions for him like with Rosalina. I asked him if he remembered my mother. At first, he said no, but after my third visit and refreshing his memory, he told me he remembers Rosalina and where and when he met her.

Closure also came when my dad said, "If I had known, you would have been with me." That is all I needed to hear to know that he would have loved and wanted me.

My life as I knew it had changed forever. Change had been a constant part of my life, and now I understood it more. Change was a part of this journey of mine, and without it I wouldn't be where I was today.

There was no doubt that I would one day look for my birth parents on my own, but I had never imagined I would ever find them both alive and well.

What was missing from their family tree was me. I never thought **my search for what was missing** in my life would lead me on a journey to finding myself. The void in my heart went from **emptiness to fulfillment**.

Now my family had expanded to include not only my adoptive family but both sides of my birth family. I am blessed to now be able to say I have two moms and two dads, and neither can take the place of the other. They were all put in my life at just the right time when I needed them, and they needed me.

I ask myself what is the meaning of my life, what is my purpose, and why was I given this *genetic journey*? The only answer I can come up with is that it was not about me, it was much bigger than being given up for adoption or finding my birth parents. It was about the lives I crossed during this journey which would allow me to help others through their own journey.

I would integrate into people's lives, at just the right time, such as at the orphanage, adoption, teenage years, young adult years, while searching for my birth parents, finding my birth parents, or even now while someone is reading his book, to help them with whatever they were going through in their own life, directly or indirectly.

Mission accomplished, I am proud of who I am and to have finished what I had set out to do. To show my children that I never gave up. My *unknown has turned into happiness*, and this new chapter is just the beginning. I could now choose my ending, close my chapter and not let the *unknown journey* consume me.

I learned that being adopted does not define who I am; I define me being adopted. My *search for existence* was always right there with me, and the lesson is that sacrifices are made to ensure life goes on.

Acknowledgements

First, thank you God for this journey.

Special thanks to my mom, dad, and grandmother that raised me. You all are loved and appreciated. This journey was chosen specifically for me with you in it, and *it **was well worth it.*** Thank you for being in my life!

To my husband, Cedric, and children, Carliss, Alexis, I'Layia, Jaden, and Kailani, and my grandchildren, Khiry, Jamir, Devon, Caisan, and Lei'Ani.

To all my family and friends, who kept me encouraged throughout my journey, this book is for you. Each bolded, italic phase within the story came from my Facebook family and friends who suggested titles for my book and poem.

To the ancestors, thank you.

To my birth parents, for whatever reason, thank you for giving me life. God separated us only to allow me to take this journey to find you both, and in turn, find me.

Our Ambiguous Reality
(The Same Yet Different)

On the Philippines Islands, in a Catholic orphanage, our lives crossed paths, as babies, in an unfamiliar, yet familiar place.

Our stories the same, yet so different
Our song the same tune, yet different verses
Our future the same unknown, yet with a different past
Our reality the same, yet with different hopes and dreams
Our same prayers, yet with our own tears
Our questions the same, but different answers

Who knew our lives would cross paths again, but as adults, in a familiar, yet unfamiliar place?

Our stories so different, yet the same
Our songs' verse the same, yet a different tune
Our past similar, with the same unknown future
Our hopes and dreams the same, yet our different realities.
Our tears shed, yet different prayers
Our same answers, but different questions

God knew our lives would cross paths again, but this time for a reason. Our story, song, tune, verses, future, past, reality, hope and dreams, prayers, questions, answers, and our tears are all the same, yet so different!

By,
JenniferRose   Davis

References

https://www.chanrobles.com/childandyouthwelfarecodeo
fthephilippines.htm#.XqiUZ- SWx9A

https://www.yourdnaguide.com/upload-to-gedmatch/

https://worldawayfromhome.com/the-indigenous-black-
filipinos/

https://lisalisson.com/5-things-   learned-delayed-birth-
certificate

Contact Me

If you're reading this page, you've finished reading, Finding Myself: How DNA and Genealogy Changed my Life.

If you are searching for someone, I hope my story has inspired you to never to give up.

I am available for the following:

❖ Inspirational Speak

❖ Interview for Publication and Media

❖ Host a Book Review

❖ Book Signing

❖ Share Your Story with Me; I would love to hear from you.

Visit me on my website at: www.thejenniferrose.com

E-mail: theJenniferRosebook@gmail.com
Facebook: theJenniferRose.com
Tic Tok: theJenniferRose.com
IG: @thejenniferrosebook

www.ingramcontent.com/pod-product-compliance
Lightning Source LLC
Chambersburg PA
CBHW062051270326
41931CB00013B/3035